Able Assistants for the Professional Minister

Broadman & Holman Professional Development Books recognize church ministry as a distinct profession and encourage the professional growth of church ministers by providing information to help them:

- Learn new ministry methods
- Enrich their skills as preachers, teachers, and counselors
- Enhance their administrative abilities, particularly in the area of strategic planning, accounting, and human resources management
- Improve their abilities to manage church growth
- Stay abreast of trends in ministry

The Professional Development Books Series:

- *The Issachar Factor:* Understanding Trends that Confront Your Church and Designing a Strategy for Success
- *Power House:* A Step-by-Step Guide to Building a Church that Prays
- *Eating the Elephant:* Bite-Sized Steps to Achieve Long-Term Growth in Your Church
- *The 12 Essential Skills for Great Preaching*
- *The Antioch Effect:* 8 Characteristics of Highly Effective Churches
- *The Empowered Communicator:* 7 Keys to Unlocking an Audience
- *The Empowered Leader:* 10 Keys to Servant Leadership
- *Giant Awakenings:* Making the Most of 9 Surprising Trends that Can Benefit Your Church
- *The Exodus Principle:* A 5-Part Strategy to Free Your People for Ministry
- *The Word for the Wise:* Making Scripture the Heart of Your Counseling Ministry

REVITALIZING
THE SUNDAY MORNING
DINOSAUR

REVITALIZING
THE SUNDAY MORNING
DINOSAUR

A SUNDAY SCHOOL

GROWTH STRATEGY FOR

THE 21ST CENTURY

KEN HEMPHILL

BROADMAN
& HOLMAN
PUBLISHERS

Nashville, Tennessee

Published by Broadman & Holman Publishers, Nashville, Tennessee
Acquisitions & Development Editor: John Landers
Interior Design: Steven Boyd
Printed in the United States of America

4261-74
0-8054-6174-4

Dewey Decimal Classification: 268.1
Subject Heading: SUNDAY SCHOOLS—ADMINISTRATION
Library of Congress Card Catalog Number: 96-16399

Unless otherwise noted, Scripture quotations are from the New American
Standard Bible, © the Lockman Foundation, 1960, 1962, 1963, 1968,
1971, 1972, 1973, 1975, 1977; used by permission.

Library of Congress Cataloging-in-Publication Data
Hemphill, Kenneth S., 1948–
   Revitalizing the Sunday morning dinosaur : a Sunday school growth strat-
egy for the twenty-first century / Ken Hemphill.
       p.   cm.
Includes bibliographical references.
  ISBN 0-8054-6174-4
  1. Sunday schools —Growth. 2. Church growth—Baptists. 3. Baptists—
Membership. 4. Southern Baptist Convention—Membership.
  I. Title.
  BV1523.G75H45   1996
  268'.861—dc20

  96-16399
  CIP

96 97 98 99 00 5 4 3 2 1

*To Harry Piland, Mr. Sunday School, and his wife, Pat.
Harry taught me to see the great evangelistic potential of the
Great Commission Sunday School.*

ᴈ

Contents

1. If the Sunday School Is a Church Growth Tool,
   Somebody Unplugged Mine! 1

2. Is Sunday School a Dinosaur
   in a Technological World? 17

3. Establishing a Great Commission Vision
   for the Sunday School. 33

4. Designing an Effective Sunday School 45

5. Organizing the Bible Study Program. 67

6. Designing an Effective Outreach Strategy. 93

7. The Ministry of Assimilation 113

8. The Ministry of Teaching. 131

9. Putting It Together—Keeping It Working 147

   Appendix 169

   Endnotes. 171

O N E

If the Sunday School Is a Church Growth Tool, Somebody Unplugged Mine!

*T*he Sunday School is the finest integrated church growth tool on the market today!" I have begun numerous conferences in various denominational settings with this assertion. My bold declaration has elicited responses varying from mild amusement, to incredulity, to outright scorn, to enthusiastic endorsement. Often religious educators applauded because they felt a certain sense of satisfaction and job security. Many, however, were guarded in their endorsements because they had not seen their ministry in terms of church growth. Other educators were somewhat hostile because they feared that the emphasis on church growth through the Sunday School would compromise their commitment to educational excellence. In truth, their Sunday School programs were not resulting in church growth. Many pastors stared at me blankly thinking, *If the Sunday School is a church growth tool, somebody unplugged mine!*

These pastors were unconvinced because they had never seen Sunday School function as a church growth tool. Most American churches have a form of Sunday School in place, but they have not experienced any perceptible growth through this organization.

Sunday School as a church growth tool? This sounds hard to believe when some church growth writers are predicting the demise of the Sunday School. They have labeled it a dinosaur, a relic of a past age. Some contend that the Sunday School was an important growth tool of the past, but it is facing extinction as the church enters the twenty-first century. Are they right?

Is the tool simply unplugged from its power source, or is it worn out and due to be replaced like your daddy's Oldsmobile? Are we hanging onto Sunday School like a fine antique automobile? Do we polish it and take it out for a drive down memory lane though we intuitively know that we shouldn't rely on our cherished classic for extended high-speed driving on today's church growth interstate?

This is a critical question because thousands of churches already have a form of Sunday School or small-group organization in place. We must seek to answer this question honestly, for we are investing valuable resources of money and time in the Sunday School structure. Our intention should never be to preserve an organization for the sake of sheer nostalgia; we need to find tools and organizations that will enable us to fulfill the Great Commission most efficiently. I believe that with a few adjustments aimed at modernization and contextualization, the Sunday School organization can be raised up from its growth malaise and take its place as the church growth tool of the twenty-first century. We can reanimate the behemoth of church growth.

A Brief Historical Perspective

Few would debate the significant role of Sunday School in the history of church growth. Yet we must take a glance backward to learn lessons for the future. It is my conviction that the Sunday School has not lost its effectiveness as a growth tool, but that we no longer use it for its intended purpose. A screwdriver is an effective tool when used properly but is totally ineffective at driving nails.

Building on the British model

Sunday Schools first appeared in America during the 1790s. Anne M. Boylan, in her study, *Sunday School: The Formation of an American Institution, 1790–1880*, writes, "Inspired by British examples, most [Sunday schools] were designed to provide rudimentary instruction to poor working children on their only free day of the week. Robert Raikes and other British evangelicals had pioneered this model during the 1780s by collecting children off city streets, cleaning them up, and keeping them in school for two long Sunday sessions."[1]

The British model of Sunday School was primarily a mission school aimed at providing basic education for those unable to attend public education. The earliest American Sunday schools were virtual copies of the British models, providing education and often essentials such as food and clothing to needy children. In time, the British model faded in America, and in its place arose a new type of Sunday School, taught by volunteers and offering a specifically evangelical Protestant curriculum. In the American school, reading was not an end in itself. The greater end was an evangelical interpretation of the Bible and the conversion of the pupil.[2]

Developing on evangelistic purpose

Using the Sunday School program to evangelize children is of such historic significance that Boylan devotes an entire chapter to the discussion of conversion and Christian nurture. She writes, "The earliest goal of evangelical Sunday school workers was simply to bring religious knowledge, and the behavior associated with it, to lower-class youth." But they accomplished much more: "They would also provide a foundation upon which their charges could construct moral lives. True morality, in their view, emanated from knowledge of the individual's ultimate accountability to God for his or her actions; without that knowledge, individuals had no incentive to behave correctly." There was even an evangelistic motive. "Although teachers did not expect their instruction to guarantee conversion—such an expectation would challenge the orthodox doctrine of inability—they did hope for subsequent conversions among pupils who participated in revivals and believed that Sunday school instruction would at the very least 'rectify and enlighten their consciences,' creating prudent and circumspect individuals."[3]

Denominationalism of the Sunday School

The earliest American Sunday School organizations were interdenominational and paraecclesiastical. Concern for evangelism, doctrinal purity, and a clear stand on moral issues led to the "denominationalization" of Sunday School. As children were converted through the Sunday School, there arose a greater concern to develop material to teach the unique doctrines of the various denominational groups that employed the Sunday School system through the church.[4]

Southern Baptists have played a leading role in the recent history of the denominational Sunday School movement. It is thus instructive to look at the purpose statement for Sunday School in the writings of early Baptist leaders. In 1902, E. Y. Mullins said, "The Sunday school must more and more prove a factor of power in the pastor's work. Already in many churches the *Sunday school is the chief and almost only hope for church growth* [my emphasis]. But whether in the family church, or the church among the masses of the great city, or the country church, the Sunday school will remain the most hopeful field of evangelistic endeavor."[5]

J. M. Frost, first head of the Baptist Sunday School Board, said, "The school becomes as an agency what the church makes it; is capable of almost indefinite expansion in church efficiency as a channel for the output of its energy and life. . . . As a force for study and teaching the Word of God; as a force for evangelizing and bringing lost sinners to the Saviour; as a force for instruction and education in the mightiest things claiming the attention of men; as a force for mission operation in the worldwide sense; as a force for making Christian character in men and women; and for opening the door of usefulness in a large scale."[6]

Arthur Flake, a layman who was instrumental in shaping Southern Baptist Sunday School, wrote, "The supreme business of Christianity is to win the lost to Christ. This is what churches are for . . . surely then the Sunday school must relate itself to the winning of the lost to Christ as an ultimate objective."[7]

The early architects of the Sunday School movement in America believed that the Sunday School must have a Great Commission focus. They did not believe that Sunday School could function properly without a clear and intentional strategy of evangelism. After persons were won to Christ, the Sunday School would nurture and train these new believers even as it helped mature all believers. Yet clearly the enthusiasm and energy for an effective Sunday School came from its clear evangelistic focus.

The beginning of the demise

It is my conviction that the beginning of the so-called demise of Sunday School can be traced to a time when denominations and local churches failed to use the Sunday School with evangelistic intentionality and purpose. When the design was forgotten, the Sunday School became a maintenance tool rather than a growth tool.

While holding growth conferences in diverse settings, I have asked participants, "What is the role of the Sunday School?" I usually get two answers: "Fellowship" and "Bible teaching." These are important, but fellowship and Bible teaching are not to be the stated purpose of the Sunday School if it is to function as a growth tool. The purpose of the Sunday School is to fulfill the Great Commission.

A Personal Discovery

I am a preacher's kid. In fact, I am the son of a Southern Baptist preacher. You might surmise that my earliest memories are of Sunday School. I was enrolled on the cradle roll before I was born. Sunday School was formative in my thinking and an ingrained part of my religious tradition. Yet in truth, it was not until relatively recent years that I began to think of the Sunday School as a tool for evangelism and church growth. I had simply never seen Sunday School used to grow the church.

My dad once told me that Sunday Schools in the past were more aggressive in evangelism than those I had experienced as a child. When I was nine years old our family moved from Morganton, North Carolina, to the not-too-distant town of Thomasville. It was hard to leave my church friends in Morganton and that beautiful brick church building in the foothills of the Blue Ridge Mountains for a decrepit building overlooking a lumber yard.

Soon, however, our new church experienced growth, and plans were made to relocate the church to a new site on a major road. Often Dad would pick me up from school and take me with him to inspect the progress of the building. These trips began even before the lot was cleared. Once the building was designed, it was as if it already existed in my dad's mind. One day when he picked me up he was flush with excitement. He could hardly wait for me to see the church. What I saw was hardly spine tingling—ditches with freshly poured concrete outlined by a few stakes with strings drawn down the entire length of the ditch. Workers had laid the foundation, but Dad could visualize the finished project.

He proudly led me on a tour of the sanctuary, pointing out the vestibule, the aisles, the pulpit area, and finally the baptistry. As we stood on a small knoll by the soon-to-be baptistry, he motioned to the strings outlining a much larger rectangle and pointed out to me the future sight of the educational building. He paused momentarily, as if reflecting back over his ministry, and said, "I can remember when virtually everyone we baptized into the church came through our Sunday School ministry. That's no longer the case. Truth is, I lead most of the new converts to Christ myself. For that reason they are more faithful to come to worship than Sunday School. The Sunday School is changing and I don't think it bodes well for the future." That conversation must have taken place about 1960.

Confirming Statistics

Since Southern Baptists have been synonymous with Sunday School growth, you might find a glimpse at their statistics to be informative. The chart below documents the concern that my dad felt about the changing direction in Sunday School and the impact it would have on Southern Baptist life. If you look across the columns of chart 1 below, you will notice first the incredible growth during the expansion years, 1940–60. Southern Baptist Sunday Schools nearly doubled in size during that twenty-year period. However, in the next twenty years, growth virtually stopped. Look also at the corresponding baptismal figures, and you will notice that growth in baptisms closely parallels the growth in Sunday School enrollment. From 1940 to 1960 baptisms increased by 57 percent. The change from 1960 to 1980 was only 11 percent. If you look at the updated 1990 column, you will note that "marching in place" has been the consistent refrain in recent Southern Baptist life. To put this chart in its proper historical and evangelical perspective, we should remember that virtually all mainline denominations have declined during this period when Southern Baptists have been able to maintain their numerical strength and even show some slight gains.

	1940	1960	1980	1990
Number of Churches	25,259	32,121	35,831	37,974
Membership	5,104,327	9,731,591	13,606,808	15,044,413
Baptisms	245,500	386,469	429,742	385,031
S.S. Enrollment	3,5900,038	7,382,550	7,433,405	8,009,498

Chart 1

In reading some of the Southern Baptist periodicals from the early 1960s, it appears to me that the emphasis in Sunday School changed first from evangelistic outreach to fellowship, then to quality Bible teaching. I agree that we should use Sunday School to build fellowship and provide quality Bible teaching, but when the focus of Sunday School moved away from evangelism, it ceased to function effectively as a growth tool. I believe that Sunday School is a simple-to-use, familiar, and effective, integrated church growth tool when used with Great Commission intentionality.

A Personal Encounter

As a young pastor, I inherited Sunday School programs that were well established but hardly aggressive in outreach. I pastored a rural church of 120 members, a small-town church of 700 members, and a metropolitan church of 6,000 members. In each case, when I came to the church the Sunday School was reasonably well organized in the preschool, children, and youth divisions but was essentially stagnant in the adult areas. Because none of these churches had a clear strategy for organizing the Sunday School for growth, most of the small groups had plateaued or declined over time, accurately displaying the condition of the church as a whole.

The beginning of the awakening

In the first two churches I pastored we experienced growth; it was reflected in the Sunday School attendance, but it was not driven by the Sunday School organization. The Sunday School was simply the recipient of growth, not the catalyst of growth. In these churches the growth was fueled by visitation, worship, and an aggressive youth program.

In one pastorate I stumbled over the potential for growth through the Sunday School. We had a number of young single members who were regular in worship attendance but had not attended Sunday School since they were in the youth department. We began a college and career class. To my amazement the class began to attract other young singles who had not been attending church anywhere. They were brought by friends! At that time I knew little about the growth principles of homogeneity and receptivity, but later I began to see that these accepted growth principles were inherent in the Sunday School structure.

On another occasion, we started a pastor's class for a group of median adult couples who attended our worship service but were uncomfortable in our existing Sunday School structure. In this case too, the class grew and attracted a new group of folk not previously involved in the church. Forming the new classes created a permanent growth situation. Both church membership and attendance increased and were sustained at these new higher levels. Other growth projects had produced momentary gains, but those gains had soon dissipated. Little did I know that I was discovering the value of the "New Unit Principle," which I will describe later in this chapter.

The growth discovery

I became the pastor of First Baptist Church of Norfolk in 1981. The church had recently relocated near the rapidly growing Virginia Beach area in Tidewater. A fire that destroyed the downtown plant had forced the move in the early 1970s. At the new location the church grew rapidly, peaking at an average of 550 in Sunday School attendance in 1976. It then declined slowly back to the 380 average Sunday School attendance mark that I inherited in 1981.

During the early months of my ministry at First, Norfolk, God began to give us immediate and spectacular results. People were joining the church every Sunday. This rapid growth was taxing to me and the one other staff person serving the church. After I had been serving the church for six months, my staff colleague was called to serve alongside the former pastor. Not only did we have insufficient staffing, but also we had even less money and physical resources. Before you think I am painting a bleak picture, I must be honest to tell you that I discovered one incredible asset. The church was blessed with a highly committed group of laypeople who had been praying for God to awaken the church to its potential and who were willing to work. Many of these persons had been faithfully serving in the Sunday School program for many years.

In those early months, I focused on the basics: preaching, teaching, training, and visiting. The rapid growth of the church was exciting but draining. The church outgrew my ability and energy rather quickly. I soon began to ask myself, "How do I care for the needs of all the church members and continue to reach the lost?" While I knew that God was sufficient, I had grave doubts about my own sufficiency. The needs were overwhelming. The young couples we were reaching had several small children, and the preschool was quickly overcrowded. We needed workers! We had seen many people profess Christ as Savior, but now we faced a huge discipling task. How could we organize to accomplish this massive task? I knew that if I stopped emphasizing our new visitation program, we would stop reaching the lost. My passion for the lost of Tidewater would not permit me to consider such an option even though many other tasks vied for our attention and resources.

I felt like the circus juggler who spins plates on long, pointed sticks. He gets two or three spinning, then he pauses to spin a new plate, but one of the spinning plates wobbles and falls to the ground. I would launch one new program after the other, trying to meet all the complex needs of a growing church. The core leaders responded to my desperate cries for help as they scurried to shore up the preschool or the outreach program or the discipling ministry. I'm sure the people must have felt that I was indecisive and unsure, for such was certainly the case. We were doing too many things but achieving few results. We had many programs, but they were disconnected. How could we organize the church to fulfill the Great Commission?

I began to devour church growth books in an attempt to find a means of coping with the growth that God was causing in our church. In each book I would find good ideas and helpful organizational structure, but it was disjointed in my thinking. With our limited staff and resources, I knew that I needed a more integrated tool, one that was simple to organize and manage.

The converging streams

Several events flowed together in my own experience that led to the conviction that the Sunday School, with its age-graded, small-group structure, might be the integrated growth tool for which I was searching.

With my Sunday School director, Dick Baker, I attended a Growth Spiral Conference led by Andy Anderson. As Andy described the Sunday School Growth Spiral, I began to recognize many parallels between the principles he was espousing and those in the pile of church growth books I had been reading. The parallels between Sunday School work and church growth principles were numerous and unmistakable. Then it dawned on me: I already have a single organization that embraces acknowledged church growth principles. Why should I create several more ministries to do the work Sunday School was designed to do?

I left that conference with a clear vision, and I was committed to make Sunday School the central organization for church growth. On the drive home, Dick and I talked about setting enrollment goals, establishing new teaching units, and administrating the Sunday School as a growth ministry, not just a maintenance organization.

I began with an abundance of zeal and a modicum of knowledge. Our first enrollment goal was for a net gain of 840 persons in Bible study. I enthusiastically had posters and banners made declaring that goal. Little did I know that a goal for over 60 percent net gain in a single year was impossible in a large church. With supernatural empowering and clear vision, even the impossible is achievable. We actually exceeded our growth goals for the year. We were well on our way to using the Sunday School as a growth tool.

One question still plagued me: If the Sunday School is such an effective growth tool, why are so few churches growing? Most of the churches that I knew about in our area had some small-group Bible study plan that resembled our Sunday School organization. Why were so few churches experiencing any real growth? Something was missing.

I found the missing factor in the equation when I attended a conference with Harry Piland, former director of the Sunday School division of the Baptist Sunday School Board. Piland stated that any adult Bible study class that had not attempted to lead anyone to Christ during the past year had missed their purpose for existing. He then affirmed that Sunday School must first be an evangelistic tool. Sunday School and outreach evangelism! I had never really connected the Sunday School with evangelistic outreach. I knew that it was effective for conserving the results of evangelism, but I had never seen a Sunday School designed for outreach.

The idea shocked me, and it rattled some of my finest teachers. Some were so convicted by their lack of evangelistic concern that they even considered resigning their classes. In the end, we all decided that repentance was more appropriate than resignation. Thus began the vision to give the Sunday School an evangelistic focus at First Baptist, Norfolk.

The event that allowed me to integrate my thinking about church growth and Sunday School was the opportunity to teach a course entitled "Growing an Evangelistic Church" at The Southern Baptist Theological Seminary. The course was designed to cover every phase of church growth. I required my students to read a wide range of materials from several different authors. As I was lecturing on the ratios for church growth, I was dumbfounded by the similarities between the ratios for growth described by Win Arn, one of the founding fathers of the church, and basic Sunday School principles. This discovery caused me to examine more closely basic Sunday School concepts and principles espoused by church growth authors. It was the final clue that helped me discover the evangelistic Sunday School as an integrated growth tool.

Parallels between Growth Principles and Sunday School

All church growth authors agree on principles though their methods differ. The distinction between method and principle is basic. Methods are many; principles are few. Methods are often tied to a particular setting, time, and person or group of persons; principles are timeless and universally applicable. A method that works well in an Atlanta suburban congregation might fail in a rural Kentucky church. In truth, it might not work in another Atlanta suburban congregation. Methods must always be contextualized. Yet the principles by which these congregations experience growth are the same.

Delos Miles, in his book *Church Growth: A Mighty River,* isolates six growth principles that run through the writings of virtually every church growth author. Miles states that all methodological strategies are based on these six principles of church growth: the Process Principle, the Pyramid Principle, the Receptivity Principle, the New Unit Principle, the Homogenous Principle, and the Leadership Principle.[8] I contend that these six principles of church growth are inherent in a properly designed evangelistic Sunday School.

Principle 1: The Process Principle

The Process Principle maintains that church growth is a process and not an event. As such, a process requires planning, goal setting, management of resources, and regular evaluation of results and effectiveness. Because church growth is a process, it is neither a passing fad nor is it a quick-fix program.

The need for planning, goal setting, management of resources, and the like strongly motivated me to organize our Sunday School to function as a church growth tool. The fundamentals for managing the process of growth were already in place through the Sunday School organization.

One of the great and continuing growth stories of our generation is First Baptist Church in Jacksonville, Florida. Copastors Homer Lindsay Jr. and Jerry Vines recently occupied their new 9,000-seat sanctuary debt free. Over the past fourteen years they have baptized 13,133 people, averaging 938 a year.

Recently, I asked a group of growth leaders to name the church that was doing a good job in reaching children, youth, singles, young adults, and various other categories. I was expecting them to name a different church in each category, but without exception they mentioned First, Jacksonville. This church has been a leader in many categories for years. How do they do it? How do they organize for such consistent and long-term growth? They focus on exalting Jesus and on personal soul-winning, and they organize everything through the Sunday School. Dr. Vines recently told me that he is always surprised when church growth experts trot out some new program or strategy for outreach, assimilation, or discipleship. They herald this new program as the latest innovation and the greatest need of the growing church. Yet when compared with a properly designed Sunday School, Vines notes, "They seem so complex and cumbersome when you can do it all so effectively and easily through the Sunday School."

Principle 2: The Pyramid Principle

The Pyramid Principle is discussed under several different names. It is actually a pictorial representation of growth. To enlarge the pyramid, you must first enlarge its base. The base of the pyramid is the organization structure for growth. Thus many would affirm that the base of the pyramid is the small-group structure through which Bible study, assimilation, and discipling relationships occur. Thus if we are to enlarge the attendance structure of our church on a permanent basis, we must continue to increase the number of small groups in the organizational base of our church.

The Pyramid Principle

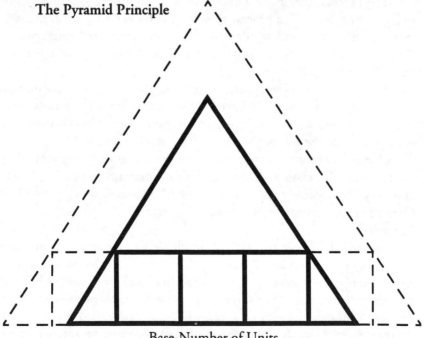

Base-Number of Units

In chapter 5 we will discuss in detail how the organizational structure for growth must be increased and is most easily expanded by developing new units and new departments in the Bible study structure of the church.

Principle 3: The Receptivity Principle

The Receptivity Principle establishes evangelism as a priority for church growth and discusses how best to present the gospel by understanding and developing natural receptivity in those to whom you are witnessing. In simple terms, the Receptivity Principle states that the church should invest most of its resources where they will return the best evangelistic harvest.

Jesus instructed His disciples to brush the dust from their feet when rejected and to go to a house that would receive them. This does not mean that the church can ignore those who reject our witness; it simply means that we must first harvest the fields that are ripe. While we are harvesting ripe fields, we can work to break down barriers to the gospel in the less receptive fields. Small groups for Bible study can often create a door of opportunity to create and foster growing receptivity for evangelistic results.

Principle 4: The Homogenous Principle

This is another principle that focuses on the evangelistic task of Sunday School. The Homogeneous Principle recognizes that the gospel witness often travels with greater receptivity through a kinship or friendship unit. Each homogenous unit in the church can become a bridge for the church to move evangelistically into the world and for the secular person to find access to the church. The growing church will sensitize its people to recognize natural homogenous groupings and utilize these as means for spreading the gospel. This principle has been fully utilized in friendship evangelism strategies. Homogeneity is the basis for a Friend Day in Sunday School. Homogeneity is the power behind the personal invitation.

The church growth movement has come under attack for its emphasis on the Homogenous Principle. This principle could be less than Christian if it fosters a spirit of racism or elitism in the church. It must never be used to justify ignoring social injustices. We can, however, reach the lost by recognizing that people look for a homogenous unit where they share some characteristics in common and to which they can belong.

For example, if you wanted to reach families living in a trailer park, you could win one family in that trailer park to Christ, organize a Bible study in their home, and invite their friends and neighbors. From here you could move to fully integrate the new Christians into the life of the church.

Once they accept Christ, they will have a new sense of homogeneity with other members of the body of Christ. In the church at Antioch (Acts 11), we have the remarkable scene of Jew and Gentile eating together. The Spirit of God had created homogeneity between two groups that had been alienated previously, but now they were united as brothers and sisters in Christ.

The small groups of Sunday School provide a natural means of using the principle of homogeneity for outreach and for developing homogenous relationships for assimilation.

Principle 5: The New-Unit Principle

Growth emanates from new units, new members, and new churches. Remember, new canes of a rose bush produce beautiful roses. Older units or groups begin to calcify. Newcomers find these old groups hard to penetrate. Churches must regularly create new groups to maintain the flow of new life. Remember the Pyramid Principle: Establishing new units expands the organizational base of the pyramid, thus empowering the Pyramid Principle.

Principle 6: The Leadership Principle

The master key of the church growth movement is leadership. To sustain meaningful growth, a church must have plenty of Great Commission-conscious leaders. This is why the growing church puts a high priority on recruiting and training leaders. The Sunday School is well designed to recruit and allocate church growth leaders.

As we look carefully at the basics of Sunday School work, we will see that all these principles are incorporated in the properly designed evangelistic Sunday School. When I examined my church in light of these principles, I realized I already had the program I needed in place. In addition, I could integrate the six principles into a single organizational strategy. I didn't have to recruit and train leadership for several programs; I could do it all through one central ministry. I didn't have to keep five different plates spinning at one time!

Revitalizing the Great Commission Mind-set

Let me close by returning to a set of questions:

- Is the Sunday School irreparably broken? No.
- Is it unplugged? Often, yes.

• What will empower the Sunday School to function as an effective church growth tool? A vision to fulfill the Great Commission.

The Sunday School must be plugged into a passion for evangelism; otherwise, it will settle into the comfort zone of a maintenance organization. By ignoring the evangelistic potential of the Sunday School, we have reduced Sunday School to a stagnant pool of introverted groups that look primarily to their own needs and interests and ignore the plight of the unsaved.

Your Sunday School does not have to remain stagnant! It can give your church the most effective Great Commission tool ever designed if it focuses on evangelism and if its purpose statement is clearly understood by all those who work and participate in it.

The Six Principles of Sunday School Growth

1. The Process Principle: Church growth is a process, not an event.

2. The Pyramid Principle: If you want to grow, enlarge your base.

3. The Receptivity Principle: Invest the most resources where they will return the best evangelistic results.

4. The Homogeneity Principle: The gospel witness often travels with greatest receptivity through a kinship or friendship unit.

5. The New Unit Principle: New units that enlarge the organization bring growth.

6. The Leadership Principle: To sustain meaingful growth, a church must have plenty of Great Commission-conscious leaders.

૨ٯ

Is Sunday School a Dinosaur in a Technological World?

We have always had a certain fascination with dinosaurs. I'm old enough to remember some of the early movies starring the behemoths of a bygone days. Some, you may recall, were innocuous lizards greatly magnified by a close-up lens. They were larger than life, but hardly frightening. Others were fairly cumbersome and patently fake mechanical monsters that waddled onto the screen with little dexterity. Yet, as children, we were wide-eyed with wonder as they trampled buildings, devoured slow pedestrians, and battled jet planes. In recent days we have witnessed an amazing growth in the popularity of dinosaurs. Today's screen dinosaurs are much more realistic and mobile than their predecessors. One dexterous monster has had the audacity to go one-on-one with Charles Barkley, the basketball star.

Dinosaur mania hit an all-time high with the box-office smash *Jurassic Park*. In the somewhat unlikely plot, modern-day dinosaurs are born from preserved prehistoric DNA. Millions of dollars are at stake since the dinosaurs are the central attraction in a theme park to end all theme parks. Yet it soon becomes clear that the animals are out of place in this technological age. They are relics from a time that no longer exists.

Some church growth writers and speakers think the Sunday School organization is a dinosaur. At a recent church growth conference where I was on the program, another speaker actually used the words "relic" and "fossil" when talking about Sunday School.

Before we can go further in discussing a Sunday School for the twenty-first century church, we must honestly answer the charge: Sunday School and other traditional growth structures are little more than the DNAs of growth strategy having no more viability in a technological society than a resurrected dinosaur in *Jurassic Park*.

Why Such Poor Results?

The first question we must pose and answer is this: If the Sunday School can function as a growth tool for the twenty-first century, why are so few Sunday Schools growing? To answer this question, we must look first at church growth on a national level. Attention to the following chart will clearly show that Sunday School growth rates have slowed in many denominational groups.

Year	American Baptist Churches USA	Assemblies of God	Church of Nazarene	Southern Baptist Convention	United Methodist Church
1920	—	4,839	50,397	1,926,610	4,324,458
1923	—	40,000	88,946	2,381,717	4,857,429
1955	969,007	805,182	582,475	6,641,715	6,810,661
1960	1,003,419	974,823	671,174	7,382,550	7,132,422
1965	917,990	1,012,932	746,325	7,659,638	6,902,438
1970	741,664	1,064,631	839,943	7,290,447	5,924,464
1980	N/R	1,389,505	879,756	7,433,405	4,222,229
1985	395,381	1,442,640	815,131	7,960,796	N/R
1990	299,609	1,403,168	860,099	8,009,498	N/R
1992				8,262,521	

First we should note that we would be hard pressed to make a case for authentic church growth in the last several decades. I do not mean to imply that there are not pockets of explosive church growth; what I do mean to imply is that as a whole, the evangelical church in America is not growing at the same pace as our population. Total membership of evangelical churches in America increased by 28 percent from 1960 to 1990, while population increased by 39 percent. U.S. population is rapidly outpacing evangelistic results. Thus, in one sense we might conclude that Sunday School as a growth tool has reflected the lack of evangelistic growth in the church at large. While this understanding may give proponents of Sunday School some solace, it hardly makes a case for the Sunday School structure as a growth tool for the future. We must probe deeper to find why a tool that once worked so well has seemingly come unplugged.

Yet your concern is probably on a more personal level. You are asking why your Sunday School does not seem to be fueling growth as it did in the past. You too are wondering if it must be cast into the category of interesting but useless relics. To this question we might offer several answers. Only you can determine those that apply to your specific situation.

Problem 1: Loss of evangelistic focus

I have already mentioned the historic evangelistic strategy of the Sunday School movement. Yet my experience has shown that few modern-day Sunday Schools have a clearly defined evangelistic focus or strategy. This lack of evangelistic focus and zeal also characterizes other church activities. We have lost our passion for evangelistic outreach, and this has clearly reduced the effectiveness of our Sunday Schools.

Anne M. Boylan, in her study of the history of the Sunday School movement, observes that the distinctively American contribution to the Sunday School movement was our use of Sunday School as an evangelistic tool. She writes, "Sunday school organizers were often well aware of the need to employ 'aggressive' means 'for reaching the masses' who did not attend regular churches." This new focus on evangelism determined the organization and structure of Sunday School in America.[1]

The loss of the evangelistic focus of the Sunday School rendered many of the original organizational strategies nonsensical. For example, if we conclude that Sunday School's primary purpose is to foster fellowship among believers, creating new units by dividing large classes doesn't make sense to the participants. That is why we hear the familiar refrain, "Why would they ask us to split our class? We are just now developing good fellowship." Such matters as age grading and promotion of pupils are meaningless if the Sunday School's primary purpose is fellowship.

If Sunday School's primary purpose is quality Bible teaching, there is little reason to have small classes and create new units. "Good Bible teachers" are few. If our focus is on quality Bible teaching, we should put all the adults in a few classes and let our master teachers lecture. Many churches do exactly this.

The pastor of an independent church came to talk with me about our Sunday School structure in Norfolk. His church was among the largest of the independent churches in our state, yet attendance had plateaued at about one thousand. Because he wanted to reach lost people, he was researching church growth. He was paying particular attention to other independent churches similar to his. He related to me that, with few exceptions, he had found that most large independent churches had been unable to break the 1,000-attendance barrier. He concluded that the primary factor was the dependence on the large sanctuary Bible class, and the failure to multiply small units for adult Bible study. They had focused on quality Bible study and had failed to understand many of the small-group dynamics that fuel growth and maintain intimacy. He came to me because he wanted to discover the method for multiplying units in Sunday School and make his Sunday School a more evangelistic organization.

Focusing on evangelism through the Sunday School has a domino effect. One thing leads to another: a strategy for creating new units, appropriate grading for all groups, regular reorganization, developing optimum-size classes, and other such factors that enable the Sunday School to be a growth tool.

Problem 2: Loss of emphasis and commitment

Growth results waned as the emphasis in Sunday School moved away from evangelism. Many pastors lost their enthusiasm for Sunday School. The early architects of Sunday School growth never doubted that the pastor was the key leader of the Sunday School. Some referred to him simply as the pastor or chief officer of the Sunday School. Early Sunday School books devoted large sections to discussing the role of the pastor in Sunday School. Some even questioned his worthiness to be pastor if he ignored the Sunday School.

In 1909, William E. Hatcher, pastor of First Baptist Church of Richmond, Virginia, wrote, "A minister who cannot thoroughly identify himself with his Sunday school ought not to be a pastor. Unfitness for service in this cardinal branch of Christian activity amounts to a disability. To be useless in that department of church work which has to do with the study of the Scriptures and with the salvation of the young is to offer an overwhelming argument against one's worthiness of a pastoral charge."[2] We might question Hatcher's conclusion, but we could hardly question his conviction that the pastor's leadership was essential to the success of the Sunday School.

Today many pastors do not view themselves as the chief officer of the Sunday School. Many view their role almost entirely in terms of worship, leadership, and pastoral care. Some are convinced that church growth is built on great worship, and they pour their strength into designing the worship service.

I have no quarrel with the importance of the worship service in fueling church growth. Worship and Sunday School are partners in growth, not opponents. Yet numerical growth built only through the large worship experience is often a very volatile growth. When the exciting worship leader leaves the church, many worship-only attenders look elsewhere for another great worship experience. *Once a church reaches people through the front door of worship, the church still must assimilate them into the small-group structure. Otherwise they will exit through the back door of apathy.*

Some pastors consider the Sunday School the domain of professional educators. Pastors often receive little seminary training about the work of the Sunday School, and they do not feel prepared to lead the Sunday School. Many have dreamed of the day that they could afford to employ a professional educator to run the Sunday School. But many pastors will never lead a multiple-staff church. Most churches are single-staff churches. Thus if the Sunday School program is to work effectively, the pastor must assume leadership. Yet even in the larger churches with specialized educational staffs, the Sunday School will not function as a powerful growth tool if the pastor does not provide leadership. The people will usually make the greatest commitment to that which the pastor gives greatest emphasis. Laypersons commit to serve in the Sunday School when they see that this is their pastor's priority.

Problem 3: Loss of vision for the total work of the Sunday School

A well-organized Sunday School integrates outreach, assimilation, and teaching. This Great Commission vision for the Sunday School gives it the necessary balance to function properly.

Many Sunday School programs have failed to produce growth results because they lack vision for the total work and consequently lose balance. If the Sunday School majors only on fellowship, it may help the church assimilate new members, but it will be ineffective at outreach. This will cause the structure to calcify and will, in time, render it ineffective at assimilation. If the focus is only on evangelism, the Sunday School could then ignore the assimilation and discipling needs of believers already involved. These believers will not be nurtured and matured, and thus they will lose the spiritual energy to reach lost people. Here again, the Sunday School starts to calcify.

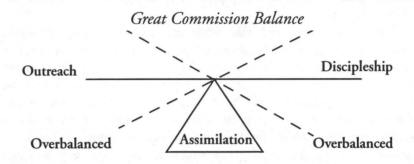

Some churches and denominations operate Sunday School only for children. They ignore its potential for reaching, assimilating, and developing adult believers. They overlook the need for continual growth among all believers.

The recent fascination with cell-group Bible studies for adults has found its strongest adherents in denominational groups without effective adult Sunday Schools. Many of these churches have discovered adult Bible study through cells. They are amazed to find they can involve many adult worshipers in small-group Bible study.

Robert Logan, a proponent of cell groups, proposes 25 percent of worship attendance in home Bible studies as a challenging goal for most churches.[3] Yet in the Southern Baptist Convention, where Sunday School has always included a strong emphasis on adults, the average church will have 85.3 percent of their worship attendance in small-group Bible study through Sunday School. If we assume that Logan is referring only to adult membership in small-group Bible study, Southern Baptist churches would compare well with 50.9 percent of adult attenders in regular small-group Bible study.[4]

I am not attempting to make a case at this point for Sunday School as opposed to cell groups. I will discuss the advantages and disadvantages of both in chapter 5. I am simply illustrating the impact of a loss of vision for the total task of the Sunday School.

Problem 4: Dismantling the component parts

Many Sunday School programs have been rendered ineffective by the dismantling of components that are vital to a growing Sunday School. For example, in the past many church buildings were built with a large department assembly room surrounded by smaller classrooms. More recent buildings often omit the departmental assembly room, viewing it as a waste of space.

While the departmental meeting may not be critical to the success of the Sunday School, the departmental organization is vital. Without a clear understanding of the critical role of this particular component, some churches did away not only with the space but the organizational principle as well. This lead to a breakdown in communication and team spirit.

Many early Sunday School programs were designed around strict age grading, accompanied by the annual promotion of children and adults alike. The promotion of adults has always been a difficult task to accomplish. Thus many churches gave up on adult promotion, which ultimately impacted the age-grading system for the Sunday School. Once this component part was removed, there was no effective manner for counteracting the stagnation that normally occurs in the small-group structure of any church. Thus the Sunday School calcified into small cliques that virtually prohibited the entry of new members.

Soon after I coauthored the book, *Growing an Evangelistic Sunday School,* I was invited to speak at a North Carolina church. The pastor asked me to teach my new book to all of his Sunday School leadership. He was preparing the church to enter a new facility on a seven-acre plot of land a few miles from the original church. He knew that the new facility would give them a greater opportunity to reach new families, but he also recognized that the church was not prepared for this influx of new members.

I had been speaking for about an hour to a rather dispassionate gathering of leaders when an elderly lady stopped me midsentence.

"Why did you write this book?" she asked.

I was clearly startled. Was she afraid that I was going to get rich on royalties?

Sensing my confusion she clarified her question. "You haven't said anything new in this book. I heard most of this when I was a young lady working in the Sunday School."

I couldn't argue with her perceptive conclusion, so I responded, "Did this church ever do all the things we're talking about tonight?"

She immediately replied, "Why, of course. I can remember when we promoted every year and had regular teacher's meetings and enrollment drives."

Calmly I asked why and when they had stopped doing the basics of Sunday School. They weren't sure why, but they had a clear memory of the "when."

It suddenly dawned on our participants that the dismantling of the component parts of the Sunday School organization corresponded with the beginning of their numerical decline. They still had a form of Sunday School, but it was greatly dismantled and clearly ineffective as a growth tool.

May I offer a little disclaimer at this point? I am not arguing for a return to the "good ole days." I am simply asserting that we must understand the dynamics that made Sunday School one of the finest integrated growth tools ever designed, and then we must contextualize and contemporize these dynamics to fit the needs of the churches of the twenty-first century.

Problem 5: Lack of a clear purpose statement

Once a Sunday School loses its emphasis on fulfilling the Great Commission, all programs start to flounder. Leaders and members no longer have a clear sense of the purpose of the Sunday School. Every Sunday School needs a clear purpose statement. We must be able to articulate why the Sunday School exists and what we expect it to accomplish. Could your Sunday School leaders write a clear and concise purpose statement? Would it include outreach?

Rick Warren, pastor of Saddleback Community Church, argues passionately that a clear understanding of purpose is a critical component of church vitality. His recent book describing the strategy of his church is aptly titled *The Purpose Driven Church*. Rick's premise is correct—the church must understand its purpose. Loss of purpose has crippled many churches and Sunday Schools.

Problem 6: Fear of innovation

We no longer live in the 1940s or 1950s. We are dealing with a new set of dynamics that has changed the playing field for the church today. Things have changed. Pluralism, urbanization, increased mobility, more women in the workforce, and lack of commitment impact the way we do church.

Most churches must contextualize their programs to fit dynamics of the local congregation. Churches must cling to the principles of Sunday School work but change their methods. Churches that fear innovation and change will stagnate. They will find that their Sunday School is a relic—little more than a feeble attempt to resurrect prehistoric DNA.

This book is not about resurrecting the past; it is about reengineering your Sunday School to become an integrated growth tool for the twenty-first century.

Could Sunday School Still Work?

The question, "Could Sunday School still work?" makes a presumption that I do not share. It presumes that the Sunday School no longer works as a growth tool. We could first point to numerous examples of great churches of all sizes that have been built on a basic Sunday School model. One of the largest Sunday Schools in America is at First Baptist Church in Jacksonville, Florida. They are presently averaging over six thousand attendees in Sunday School. Their school is basic but extremely well done. First Baptist Church in Orlando; Bellevue Baptist Church in Memphis; First Baptist, Woodstock, Georgia; First Baptist, Snellville, Georgia; First Baptist, Springdale, Arkansas; Hyde Park Baptist in Austin; First Baptist in Dallas; First and Second Baptist in Houston, and a host of other successful churches have been built on basic Sunday School models. In fact, at a recent gathering of the largest churches in Southern Baptist life, I found that over 90 percent were built on basic Sunday School principles and strategies. All of these churches had other fine programs, but they are basically organized to grow through the Sunday School.

Lest you think Sunday School is only a growth tool for the largest churches, I maintain that it works effectively in the small to moderate size churches of different ethic groupings. Look, for example, at Arlington Park First Baptist Church in Dallas, Texas; Estrella de Belen in Dallas, Texas; Temple Jerusalem in Victoria, Texas; and Carolina Memorial Baptist in Thomasville, North Carolina.

Pat Pajak became the pastor of Tabernacle Baptist Church in Decatur, Illinois, in January of 1991. That year the church averaged 165 in twenty-two teaching units. Pat began to build the church through the Sunday

School. In January of 1996 the church was averaging 561 in Sunday School with sixty-one teaching units. They have now implemented three Sunday School hours on Sunday morning (8:15, 9:30, and 10:45). They are presently preparing to implement a Bible study program on Saturday evening.

Morningside Baptist Church in Valdosta, Georgia, has had a similar growth story. During the last five years, average attendance in Sunday School has grown from 478 to 630, while teaching units have grown from fifty-one to eighty-seven. Baptisms during this five-year period have averaged seventy-nine. The secret to this growth success has been a well-organized Sunday School coupled to an aggressive visitation program.

Sunday School has been used as a growth tool by churches from many denominations. Kennedy Smartt, a Presbyterian minister, tells of his discovery of the Sunday School as an evangelistic tool. He refers to the sterile and dying Sunday Schools in many settings that are designed to serve the "select of the elect." He then goes on to write about seven keys to a growing Sunday School.[5]

Those who have predicted the demise of the Sunday School might also want to consider the opinion of men who have been involved in church growth research. Kirk Hadaway, in his well-documented book, *Church Growth Principles: Separating Fact from Fiction,* looked at the role of Sunday School. He writes, "Is there a strong relationship between the quality of Sunday School programming and church growth? The answer is yes." He notes that 84 percent of growing churches rated their adult Sunday School as excellent or good, as compared to only 56 percent of plateaued churches and 46 percent of declining churches. In addition he discovered that 78 percent of plateaued churches that managed to break out of their plateaued situation reported an increased emphasis on the Sunday School.[6]

Leith Anderson, when looking at the church of the twenty-first century, predicted that the traditional church will be one of the major growing segments of the twenty-first century. He argues that we have ignored America's growing interest in the traditional, the attempt to recapture yesterday. He states that the traditional churches will need to incorporate many contemporary elements and do the traditional with a high level of excellence.[7]

Along the same lines, Elmer Towns writes, "Growing churches today are returning to traditional laws of Sunday School growth and implementing these principles into their ministry."[8]

George Barna has recently noted that developed properly, the Sunday School could be a valuable tool for reaching non-Christians. This statement was fortified by a graph that demonstrated that thirteen million non-Christian adults attend Sunday School. Sunday School has clearly provided a key entry point for unsaved adults. Once enrolled, receptivity is easily developed.[9]

Church Involvement and Satisfaction

Developed properly, Sunday School could be a valuable tool for reaching non-Christians:

Millions of Adults Attending Sunday School Regularly*

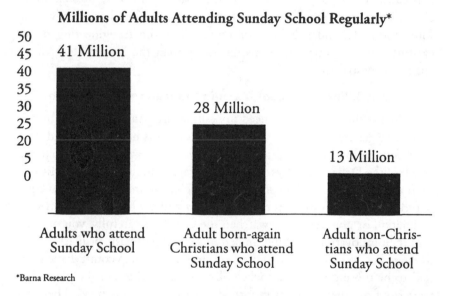

*Barna Research

Why Sunday School Is the Growth Tool of the Future

In contrast to those who call Sunday School a dinosaur, a relic of the past, I believe it is the growth tool of the future. Here are nine reasons why you should consider Sunday School as an integral part of your strategy as you marshal your tools to reach your community and the nation for Christ.

Reason 1: Sunday School provides a centralized and simplified strategy

As your church grows, the need to centralize and simplify will become more critical. It is much easier to find the leadership for a single organization that can fulfill the threefold task of outreach, assimilation, and teaching than staffing three or more different organizations. The centralizing of our Great Commission work in a single organization will simplify the administrative work for every size church. *You can't do everything in Sunday School, but you can organize to do much of your growth work through the Sunday School.*

Reason 2: Sunday School is familiar

In our rapidly changing culture it is comforting to know that some things are stable. Most people who have any church background or experience have been involved in a Sunday School program of some kind. Thus it is easier to get people involved both as participants and workers in an organization with which they are familiar. Many churches already have some form of Sunday School structure. Thus the reengineering of an existing structure may cause less resistance than the introduction of an entirely new structure.

Reason 3: Sunday School is a solid foundation for innovation

No one should deny the need to be innovative in order to reach each successive generation. Yet meaningful innovation is best constructed on a solid foundation of basic principles. Several years ago Tom Landry, the coach of the Dallas Cowboys, changed the face of football forever. His formations were new. He had so many people going in motion it not only befuddled the opposition, the referees weren't sure whether they had seen a violation or not. Yet if you watched the Cowboys carefully, you noticed that their innovation was built on better execution of basic principles. The linemen had to be more disciplined to listen for the snap count. Execution had to be more precise. And when all was said and done, the plays that were run from these innovative formations were still basic plays. They still ran the ball up the middle, off tackle, and around the end.

Innovation is always built on the foundation of fundamental principles. Sunday School can provide that foundation for your church. A strong Sunday School is not a deterrent to innovation, it is the foundation for innovation.

Reason 4: Sunday School incorporates the six principles of church growth in one organization

When Sunday School has a clear purpose statement and is managed correctly, it incorporates those principles that most growth authors agree to be fundamental—the Process Principle, the New Unit Principle, the

Leadership Principle, the Homogeneity Principle, the Receptivity Principle, and the Pyramid Principle.

Reason 5: Sunday School is the natural companion to an exciting worship service

If you have discovered that people in your community are more likely to come first to a celebrative worship service, the Sunday School still provides the best method for assimilating these newcomers so that they become attached to the family. If new members are only attached to the worship leader, their attendance and commitment is often more sporadic. New members will be assimilated only as they develop intimate personal relationships through small-group contact.

You will also probably encounter some people who will find it easier to enter your church through a small homogeneous group rather than through the large worship service. They may fear the large number of people who gather for worship. The Sunday School will not only provide a more personal entry point for such people, it will actually fuel the growth of your worship service. Those people who enter first through Sunday School will ultimately become involved in your worship experience.

Joseph Dennis recently completed his doctor of ministry degree at Fuller Theological Seminary. He selected as his topic, "Building Bridges to Baby Boomers through the Sunday School." He writes, "The Sunday School has the opportunity to build a bridge to Baby Boomers like no other organization within the church by meeting their needs through the application of the Word of God. Since the Bible is the textbook for the Sunday School, this should be attractive to Baby Boomers who desire to study it, not only for what it meant when it was written, but how it applies now."[10]

Reason 6: Sunday School gets people involved in service

People who become involved in the church's ministry will progress more quickly in their spiritual walk and will have a deeper commitment to the church. The Sunday School provides many opportunities for people with differing gifts to be involved in ministry. Win Arn taught us that involvement of a large number of persons in service was a prerequisite to effective and lasting church growth. In his book, *The Church Growth Ratio Book*, he argues that the growing church needs sixty tasks for every one hundred members.[11]

Reason 7: Sunday School provides the small-group experience every Christian needs

Everyone who comes to your church asks these two questions:

• Am I wanted?

• Am I needed?

Involvement in a small group says, "You are wanted; you belong." Opportunities for service made available through the small-group structure of the Sunday School say, "You are needed." Christians were never intended to live in isolation. Jesus began His ministry by establishing a small group of followers.

Reason 8: Sunday School is not tied to a single personality

Growth through worship is often tied to the personality and skills of the worship leader. When that gifted worship leader leaves, the crowd often falls off. It is easier to draw a crowd than to build a church. As a general rule, the way you reach people is the way you must keep them. If you reach them through big events and powerful personalities, you are always struggling to produce bigger and bigger events. If a church across town produces a more spectacular event, those you attracted with spectacular events will leave you for the church across town. A church built on the small-group structure is founded on the solid rock of relationships, not on personalities or events.

Reason 9: Sunday School has a proven track record

Everyone interested in church growth has seen methods burst on the scene with spectacular results. Do you remember the bus ministries of the 1960s? What about the youth musicals and touring youth choirs? They no longer pack church as they did in the 1970s. Someday people may remember the celebrative worship services of the 1990s. Just remember, many churches that once prospered on trendy methods are now shells of their former glory because they never assimilated the people they reached with their trendy methods.

Year in and year out, the Sunday School structure, properly used, has given solid results. If we were to do away with Sunday School, we would have to build something very much like it to replace it. Why not build innovative strategies on the proven historic principles of Sunday School growth?

Looking Ahead

Sunday School is no dinosaur. Its demise in some congregations and denominations can be traced to several causes, chiefly a loss of evangelistic fervor. Once churches lost their vision for Sunday School as a church growth tool, they could see no significance in the component parts in and of themselves. Thus the integrated growth tool was slowly dismantled.

Sunday School, when designed with a clear evangelistic purpose, becomes a vital integrated church growth tool for today's church. It is simple to use and provides many advantages for churches of any size.

This raises another question: How can we create a Great Commission vision that will unify the Sunday School? This will be our focus in the next chapter.

ða

THREE

Establishing a Great Commission Vision for the Sunday School

*M*ost churches that have come to life after a period of virtual inactivity point to a supernatural awakening with the accompanying renewal of vision for fulfilling the Great Commission. Recent church growth authors have reminded us of the power of vision to ignite growth. Yet, this is clearly not a new discovery.

Almost every evangelical church today began because someone had a vision for building a community of people who could fulfill the Great Commission. Vision led them to buy land and to build buildings. Vision led to purposeful evangelistic activity and to sacrificial giving and service. However, once churches realize their original dream, they often become complacent and even forget that they were once a visionary people. They then tend to live in the glow of past greatness rather than look for new opportunities. *When church conversation focuses on the greatness of the past more than the potential of the future, the church is destined for further decline.*

If you are in an established church, you must first lead your church to renew its vision to move toward effective growth. You must connect with the vision of the past, then help your people "renew the dream."

If you are in a new church, you should be sure to saturate everything you do with a Great Commission vision. To do so, you must establish a clear vision, keep that vision before your people, and renew it regularly;

otherwise your church will slip into complacency and then into mediocrity.

The Bible is replete with examples of great works that began as God communicated His vision to a willing and obedient people. It is not an exaggeration to state that no great movement of God has ever begun without a vision from God received and implemented by a willing people. The first step to resurrecting the dinosaur of church growth potential latent in your church is to develop a Great Commission vision.

Vision, however, does not develop in a vacuum. I have consulted with churches that had adopted vision statements, had shared them through preaching and through announcement in their printed materials, but had seen few results. Vision that ignites growth must emerge from renewed passion. This passion motivates people to act. Passion fuels church growth.

Once the church has renewed its passion, a clearly articulated vision statement can focus the power of passion the way a laser beam focuses the power of light. Passion is reborn when there is an authentic encounter with the living God. When we have a passion to know Him and to be known by Him, we will share His passion for winning the lost to faith in Him. *Authentic church growth is fueled by a passion to see the Great Commission fulfilled.*

Why speak of Great Commission vision, or Great Commission passion? Why add the words *Great Commission?* Let's look at that question.

Why Anchor Vision in the Great Commission?

Here are some practical and biblical reasons for developing a Great Commission consciousness and for anchoring church growth vision to the Great Commission.

Great Commission vision has a biblical focus

Many pastors and laypersons alike are often dismayed to discover that many members of their churches do not want to talk about church growth. They will often argue that the emphasis on numbers in church growth is not very spiritual. It has always intrigued me that many of the people who make such an argument have never been accused by their peers as being overly sensitive to spiritual matters in other arenas.

Still other people may object to numerical church growth based on their fear of losing the intimacy that they have come to enjoy in their small church or Sunday School class. Although it is impossible to dilute true biblical fellowship through numerical growth, it is often hard to dislodge such emotional arguments when talking about church growth.

If, however, the church focuses on fulfilling the Great Commission, it is difficult to mount any serious objection to such a focus without revealing the true selfish and carnal motives that are behind the desire to keep the church small or a particular class together. Simply put, Great Commission vision is biblically based. It focuses church growth on the Great Commission. This is why it is difficult for Christians to oppose growth activities based on the Great Commission.

In addition, Great Commission vision ensures that our motives for growing the church are genuine. Pride will not produce authentic or balanced growth. When a church wants to grow only to keep up with the First Church or some booming church of another denomination, the motive is wrong and the results will not last. *Obedience to the Great Commission, not church growth, is the appropriate goal for any church. Church growth results from obedience to the Great Commission.*

Great Commission vision ensures supernatural empowering

Someone told J. N. Barnette, "I would rather have a good Sunday school than a big one." Barnette's reply was classic: "The statement, I had rather have a good Sunday school than a big one, comes from a heart that has been deceived by the forces of evil, from a heart of indifference, or from a heart that is seeking to cover failure with pious platitudes."[1]

We have all heard the vision-destroying objections:

• We don't have the space.
• We don't have the money.
• We can't staff the classes we have now.
• We can't do what big churches do.
• We'll lose our fellowship.
• We've tried that before.
• We've never tried that before.
• I would rather have a good Sunday School than a large one.

Yes, we do face vision-destroying objections when we attempt anything big for God. We must not let small thinking deter us from obedience to the Great Commission. How then can we answer such objections without wrangling over financial projections and growth demographics? Keep the focus on supernatural empowering.

The biggest deterrent to growth in most churches is lack of confidence in God's supernatural power to grow His church. We are obsessed with our own responsibility to find resources for growth. When our natural resources seem limited, our vision shrinks and we accept mediocrity. We can't grow the church, but God can! We don't have the resources, but He does!

A few years ago I was intrigued by the title on the back page of a Christian magazine. It read, "I never thought I would be carnal." The author shared that she had always thought of carnal behavior as that which occurs when a Christian goes back into the world. She then realized that she could be carnal while doing her work in the church. Carnality, she noted, was the attempt to do supernatural work with natural strength. How often does carnality rear its ugly head when we are talking about how we can fulfill the Great Commission?

Before Jesus commissioned His disciples to go into all the world and make disciples, He assured them that all authority in heaven and on earth had been given to Him. After giving the Great Commission, He reminds them that He will be with them always as they work to fulfill the Commission. The problem with the average Christian and the average church is that we are working for God. The world is not impressed! If the world were to see God working through us, then they would be impressed.

The Lord Jesus gave us His assurance that He would build His church (Matt. 16:18); He promised us that He would be with us as we join Him in Great Commission work. Our resources for growth are as unlimited as God is. The greatest force in the universe is the church that is alive with the power of God. The gates of hell itself cannot stand against the church empowered by the resurrected Lord.

We will never have a Great Commission vision if we let our own resources and abilities limit the size of our vision. Jesus would not have given us a spiritual task and a world vision had He not intended to give us supernatural empowering. Trying to do spiritual work in human empowering results in the sin of carnality. The fleshly individual or church will never accomplish anything for God. Growth is stifled by our lack of biblical understanding of the nature of God and the nature and empowering of the church.

The average church is average because it operates as if Jesus had never been raised from the dead. It has forgotten His promise to send the Holy Spirit to empower disciples of every generation to do greater works than He did (John 14:12). A vision based in the Great Commission begins with promised supernatural empowering. This promise, when understood, creates expectancy and engenders a "can-do" attitude. It is not the arrogant we-can-do attitude, but the assured He-can-do attitude. He can supply all our needs![2]

Great Commission vision assures us of a balanced strategy

Balance is assured because the Great Commission is a biblical method given by the Lord Himself. The overarching concern of the Great Commission is the "making of disciples." Only by making disciples will the church complete the work of Christ. Since disciple-making is a supernatural work, the church must follow a God-given strategy. The Lord gave us a threefold strategy outlined by the words *going, baptizing,* and *teaching.* Notice the three-step sequence of disciple-making:

1. Going=Evangelizing
2. Baptizing=Assimilating
3. Teaching Obedience=Discipling

The church must first declare the good news of the gospel to the lost world that is blinded by sin. Second, after a person has made a personal commitment to Christ, he or she must then be baptized into the life of a local congregation. I often translate the word *baptism* as assimilation. New believers must be incorporated into the life of a New Testament church. Birth should occur in the context of a nurturing family, whether physical or spiritual. Evangelistic concern that does not focus on congregationalizing the convert is not New Testament evangelism. Third, a Great Commission strategy must teach new converts to observe all that Christ taught. Not only is this a balanced strategy, but it is a reproductive strategy—it will create a continuous cycle of disciple making.

The Great Commission is so straightforward and balanced, we must wonder why we continually think we can improve on it. I observed that when a church has a balanced Great Commission approach, that church has natural and healthy growth. Think of balanced growth as a seesaw. Going is on one side; teaching is on the other. Assimilation is the fulcrum.

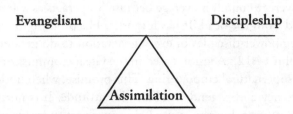

When a church gets unbalanced to either side, natural growth is inhibited. The leaders of some churches have a passion for soul-winning; they put all their emphasis on reaching people but have little or no strategy for assimilating new converts and for discipling existing believers. We could illustrate this church in this manner:

Discipleship

Evangelism

Assimilation

- Statistical records may show that this church has evangelized many people. Yet upon close examination you will notice that all attendance statistics remain relatively flat or may show a decline.

- This church appears preoccupied with numbers. They will be accused of counting nickels and noses.

- Church members often complain that their pastor neglects their needs.

- The self-delusion of this church is that it claims to be concerned about "souls," but its failure to assimilate and nurture new believers indicates little genuine concern for individuals.

On the other side of the coin, some churches put all their emphasis on discipling believers. Some have taken this approach in an overreaction against the evangelism-centered church. Others have taken such an approach simply because they want to avoid the hard work of evangelism. Some churches who have lost their biblical foundation have been overly influenced by the mistaken hope that everyone will get to heaven one way or another. We could illustrate this church in this manner:

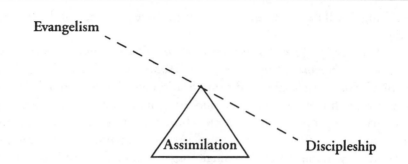

- This church often belittles numerical growth through conversion with the claim to be interested in quality, not quantity.

- Once again enrollment and attendance figures will be plateaued or declining.

- This church tends to become cliquish because of the exaggerated emphasis on fellowship and discipleship. This will generally create stagnancy in the small-group structure.

- The self-delusion of this church is that it prides itself on being concerned about discipleship, but in truth it is not developing authentic disciples. The goal of all discipling is to form the image of Christ in believers. How could anyone be considered discipled who manifests no concern for reaching lost persons. Jesus declared that He came to seek and save the lost.

Sunday School—The Primary Great Commission Tool

I have already suggested that the Sunday School, correctly postured, could be the most powerful integrated growth tool for the church of the twenty-first century. Before you dismiss my thesis out of hand, let me suggest eight good reasons to use your Sunday School organization to help you implement your Great Commission strategy.

Reason 1: The Sunday School has the organizational structure to hold together the three elements of the Great Commission—evangelizing, assimilating, and discipling. I'm not suggesting that we can do everything necessary to fulfill the Great Commission in one hour, but we can do virtually everything through one organization.

The Sunday School properly organized is a small-group network that involves every age group of the church. For this reason it can function as the organizational structure for reaching, assimilating, and teaching. I will devote an entire chapter to discussing each of these components.

Reason 2: Tying together the three elements of the Commission in the Sunday School simplifies planning, resource allocation, and calendaring. The principles of centralization and simplification are vital to a church of any size. Every church faces crises in allocating its resources, both financial resources and people resources. Many churches have stalled in an attempt to reach their community because they simply could not staff their various programs. Working through a single organization will not lessen your needs for trained leaders. You will still need people involved in outreach, inreach, and discipleship. However, working through a single organization will greatly simplify your work.

Centralization will simplify training and allocation and cut down on areas of duplication. For example, record keeping and publicity can now be centralized. You can also cut down on planning and organizational meetings by gathering all the Great Commission leaders at one time and then breaking into specialty work groups. Until you centralize your Great Commission strategy, you will always feel like the juggler who attempts to keep more and more plates spinning atop pointed sticks. Without feverishly running from stick to stick, the plates begin to wobble and ultimately fall to the ground. We will look at centralizing your planning and resource allocation in greater detail in chapter 9.

Reason 3: Organizing through the Sunday School helps create a team spirit. In many churches I often get the feeling that some tension exists between those involved in the various Great Commission tasks. Persons involved in evangelism can become cliquish, virtually excluding church members who do not appear to have equal zeal for the lost. Those involved in discipling tasks sometimes develop a sense of spiritual superiority that seems to say, "I have arrived spiritually." Since the assimilation process is unseen and unorganized in many churches, those who are committed to such tasks can often be overlooked in the overall strategy of the church and thus made to feel unimportant.

Even in the best of conditions, when these three functions are not centralized through a single organization like the Sunday School, they can become competitive rather than cooperative. Leaders in charge of their respective programs often attempt to recruit the same people for leadership positions. Many of the church disagreements that I have observed have often centered around the relative merits of a certain component part of the overall program. These arguments have developed because of a lack of team spirit and overall vision. These potential problems can be avoided by organizing the Sunday School to fulfill the Great Commission.

Reason 4: A Great Commission focus gives life to the Sunday School and thus counteracts stagnancy. One of the primary problems you will face with any organization of small groups is the tendency toward stagnancy. It is an unwritten law that small groups left alone will move toward entropy. They will become stagnant and introverted. This is true whether you have organized your small groups through the traditional Sunday School strategy or through a cell-group structure. If your small-group organization does not have an evangelistic purpose statement, your small groups will ultimately stagnate and will become a hindrance to growth rather than a tool for growth.

This may explain why many churches that have had traditional Sunday School have been enamored by the cell-group movement. They have allowed their Sunday School structure to calcify, and they are looking for a way of breathing new life into their church. Many cell-group churches have also experienced stagnation in their cell groups. The issue here isn't Sunday School versus small groups; the issue is the Great Commission focus versus a lack of focus. Without a Great Commission focus the church, whether organized through cells or traditional Sunday School structure, will stagnate.

Reason 5: The Sunday School has been vastly underutilized as an evangelistic tool. The Sunday School as a growth tool is not a fossil, but, truthfully, we have simply ceased to use Sunday School as an evangelistic tool.

Kennedy Smartt has written a refreshingly honest and confessional article on "Evangelism through Sunday Schools." He first notes that when evangelistic strategy is discussed among many Reformed and Presbyterian churches, the importance of Sunday School is commonly overlooked. He then notes that many Sunday Schools are unhealthy because they have forgotten or neglected the basics of Sunday School growth. They have forgotten to use the Sunday School as an outreach tool.[3]

Smartt is accurate in his assessment that many churches have ignored the vast potential of the Sunday School as an effective growth tool. First, we have ignored the basic truth that people come to a particular church primarily because they are invited by a friend or relative. Different growth authors have estimated that 79 percent to 86 percent of persons chose a particular church because of a personal invitation from a friend or relative.

A fully age-graded Sunday School provides a vast network of persons who, when properly trained and motivated, can bring their friends to their small group.

Those who argue that people are attracted by the large celebrative worship service are off base. *People are attracted through relationships, not events.* Events—such as the celebrative worship service or a singing Christmas tree—may provide the opportunity for church members to invite their friends to attend with them, but it is the personal invitation that works, not the event. Interestingly some growth writers argue that the "front door" of worship is already closing and that the church of the coming decades will reach the unchurched through the side door of small groups.[4]

To me, the argument over "front door" or "side door" is a nonissue. Bring your friends to church through any door possible. Different people with different needs may enter through different doors. The fact remains that you must bring them with you through the door. The small-group structure of Sunday School provides bountiful opportunities of natural networks for bringing unsaved friends. George Barna's research cited in the second chapter reveals that Sunday School does work as an entry point for the unsaved. He discovered thirteen million adult non-Christians who attend Sunday School. We don't always know how many unsaved people attend our worship services because we have no sure method of recording their attendance. The intimacy of the small-group structure of Sunday School virtually assures that you will know the unsaved persons who are attending. Sunday School in most churches is an untapped evangelistic gold mine.

Furthermore, the intimacy of a small group like a Sunday School class is more relational than a worship service. Here friendships can be made that may become a natural bridge to presenting the gospel. Such relationships are difficult to establish in a worship center of any size. Sunday School provides a family atmosphere that makes evangelism more natural. The Sunday School properly organized maximizes the positive aspects of homogeneity and receptivity, two principles that are crucial to evangelistic outreach.

The focus on evangelism through the Sunday School will have another positive effect. It will help to counteract the stagnancy that tends to calcify the small-group structure of the church. The evangelistic focus will require that you create new units and keep the small groups at a manageable size.

Reason 6: The Sunday School provides a natural context for assimilation. As physical birth is nurtured in a family setting, spiritual birth is best nurtured in a small group like that of Sunday School. The Sunday School class can become the natural family setting for the assimilation of new believers. It is small enough for the individual to be known and cared for. The new believer must sense that he or she belongs and is needed. The care leader ministry (see chap. 7) can provide one-on-one nurturing, and the Sunday School ministry can provide entry-level service opportunities.

Reason 7: The Sunday School puts Bible teaching in the center. Because it focuses on Bible teaching, the Sunday School can anchor the various components of church growth—evangelism, assimilation, and discipleship—in a sound biblical and theological base.

Various studies have shown that long-term healthy growth is dependent on sound doctrinal training. Brenton Johnson, Dean R. Hoge, and Donald A. Luidens studied the decline of the Presbyterian Church, U.S.A. They discovered that the single best predictor of church participation turned out to be belief—orthodox Christian belief. Persons who were active in their church had a well-articulated, theologically conservative understanding of God, Jesus Christ, the nature of the Bible, the Christian life, and the afterlife.[5] This finding is confirmed by a more extensive study by Roger Finke and Rodney Stark. They discovered that churches that rejected traditional doctrines and ceased to make serious demands of their followers ceased to prosper.[6]

Building your church through the Sunday School will help to ensure that your growth is based on sound biblical principles, not just on emotion and enthusiasm. While promotion and big events can play a significant role in attracting the unsaved, these promotions cannot be the substance of lasting church growth. Growth that remains will be built on the integrity of the Bible teaching ministry of your church.

Reason 8: Great Commission focus gives your Sunday School a clear purpose statement. Many Sunday Schools are ineffective because leaders and members are not always in agreement on the purpose of the Sunday School. The purpose will ultimately determine such issues as the size of classes, the creation of new units, and the strategy for grading the Sunday School. Confusion over these matters will always be present in the Sunday School that does not have a clear purpose statement. Using the Great Commission as a purpose statement will enable you to keep the Sunday School focused on a biblical strategy. This strategy was given by the Lord of the church, who Himself promised to grow the church. Thus it is endued with supernatural power.

Putting It Together

We have looked at advantages to building your Sunday School or small-group structure on a Great Commission model. This keeps the focus biblical and provides the supernatural empowering necessary for church growth. The greatest practical advantage is the balance the Great Commission provides for outreach, assimilation, and discipleship. I believe there are many advantages to organizing your Great Commission strategy through the Sunday School. I know you may still be dubious that such a lofty goal can be achieved through an organization that in many churches appears to be showing early signs of rigor mortis. I would agree that many Sunday Schools are nearly comatose, but I believe they can be shocked back to life by an infusion of Great Commission consciousness. Once revived we must look at designing them for effectiveness. Let's look at the design or redesign phase in the next chapter.

≥∂

F O U R

Designing an Effective Sunday School

When I was a child I had little patience for or interest in the design phase of a project. I was so action centered, I wanted to get right to work. If we were building a tree house, I was the first to start cutting boards and hammering nails. While others were measuring and planning, I was sawing away. Needless to say, I ended up with many useless planks that were cut to the wrong size.

I wanted to see progress. My theory was that the faster I began to build, the more quickly I could enjoy the benefits of the project. I could see myself sitting in the tree house. No one could fault my vision, enthusiasm, or work ethic, but my lack of planning often created waste. Boards would be cut prematurely and thus too short. (It really is quite difficult to glue those short pieces back together!) My dad would gently correct me by telling me that the time spent in planning would be paid back many times over.

Many churches latch onto a new idea and try to implement it immediately. They spend little time in the design phase. Soon they are frustrated. (The hard work that goes into cutting those first boards is often wasted work.) This wasted effort can have the further effect of slowing positive growth momentum. The importance of momentum in the matter of church growth cannot be overlooked. Churches tend to grow because of positive momentum and decline when the momentum shifts.

Unfortunately the downward momentum of decline tends to be a more powerful force than the upward momentum of growth. If you can picture the arduous climb of a roller coaster up the first hill and then the rapid descent of the free fall, you will get the idea. Adequate planning will allow a church to have a design that enables them to maintain positive momentum and avoid the roller coaster rides of growth and decline.

This chapter focuses on the design phase of church growth through the Sunday School. Are you tempted to skip over it and grab the hammer and saw? If so, fight back the temptation. The design phase lays the foundation for all that is to follow. I will attempt to keep it brief and practical so that it can be of value to the new church or the established one, the large church or the small one, and the urban church or the rural one.

Start by Focusing on Supernatural Empowering and Prayer

The design phase must be saturated in prayer and guided by the understanding of the resources available to the church for growth. If we begin with the biblical presupposition that church growth is both a natural phenomenon and a supernatural occurrence, we will base our design on biblical principles and take full advantage of the supernatural empowering of God.

In Matthew 16:18 we are told that Jesus promised that He would build His church. The church was divinely designed to grow, and it is super-naturally empowered to grow. Thus a second and logical presupposition is that God wants your church to grow. We have no right to decide not to grow. It would be sinful to stand in the way of God's plan to grow our church.

Our first priority is to discover His design, plan, and purpose for the church. I have found the study of the church at Antioch to be a particularly helpful study for church growth. You may find my book *The Antioch Effect: Eight Habits of Highly Effective Churches* to be a good tool for leading your church to focus on the supernatural resources available for growth.

There are four obvious advantages to designing for growth with a focus on supernatural empowering.

1. Focusing on supernatural empowering creates a can-do attitude

We have all been discouraged by the negativism that inhibits growth. You suggest a new idea, and someone responds, "We can't afford that!" You devise a new plan for increasing the number of small groups, and someone reminds you, "We don't have enough leaders to staff the groups we have now. Why should we plan for new groups?" You challenge your church or class to invite lost friends, and they complain, "We don't have enough space as it is. Why should we worry about bringing others?" Then you suggest building onto the church to allow for growth, and you're again confronted with the reminder that, "We don't have the resources."

Our negative spirit is nothing more than unbelief, and our unbelief inhibits the work of the Spirit and the flow of power. Even Jesus was able to do little in his hometown of Nazareth because of their unbelief (Mark 6:5–6). I am convinced that many churches are not growing because of the sin of unbelief. We are trying to remedy the problem of the lack of growth in most churches by finding a new model, method, or marketing strategy. But our new models and methods are not working because we have not properly diagnosed the problem for our lack of growth. We have a spiritual problem, and it will not be remedied by a new program.

Unbelief manifests itself in many ways in the church. Its most obvious manifestation is in our carnal thinking about our prospects for growth. Most of our plans reflect natural thinking, not supernatural thinking. For example, was your church budget for this year based on "what we think we can give" or "what is needed for fulfilling the Great Commission"? When approached for service, do people respond, "Oh, I could never do that" or "Let me pray about it and see what God says"?

If we listen to the conversation of most churches, we will discover the carnality of our thinking. Many churches are operating as if God had not sent His Holy Spirit to empower us to do greater things than were accomplished through His Son's earthly ministry. We answer most challenges for service based on our paltry human resources rather than God's extravagant divine resources. We're challenged to teach, but we cry that we could never do that. We're asked to witness, and we excuse ourselves by arguing that witnessing is just not natural to us. My response: "Good, we can use you. We don't need teachers who are relying on natural ability. We need teachers who teach from supernatural empowering." Witnessing isn't supposed to be natural! Its always supernatural. It was only after the Holy Spirit came upon the early disciples that they spoke with boldness.

When a church or an individual focuses on the supernatural empowering of God, it creates a can-do attitude. If God has called us to do something, He will empower us to accomplish that task. You can be certain that God has called you to fulfill the Great Commission in your community. Why not begin to do so based on His promises?

2. Focusing on supernatural empowering eliminates all so-called legitimate excuses

Many well-designed growth plans are scuttled by feeble excuses. It is easy to think of reasons we can't accomplish the Great Commission in our context. We can blame our lack of activity on our circumstances, our lack of money or leadership, our poor facility, the hardness of the spiritual soil in our community, or a myriad of other excuses. But they are all excuses!

The church at Antioch could have balked when God gave them the vision to evangelize the world (Acts 13:1–3). It seemed impossible. Travel was difficult. Such a mission would require them to give up their two best leaders, Paul and Barnabas. A missionary journey was an innovative idea that had never before been tried. This strategy might not work. They could have raised many objections. Instead, they obeyed.

When God called Moses to lead Israel out of Egyptian captivity, Moses first responded with excuses. He reminded the Lord that he was slow of speech. He may have considered himself unworthy because he was still a wanted murderer in Egypt. He could not understand how he could stand against the "god-like" Pharaoh and all his powerful magicians. This was clearly a humanly impossible task.

God answered Moses' objections by revealing Himself to Moses. He was the God of Abraham, Isaac, and Jacob. This historical reference reminded Moses of all of God's activity in the past to provide for His people. He also revealed Himself through His memorial name, I AM THAT I AM (Exod. 3:13–16). His name was a clear indication of His sovereign power to accomplish whatever He willed. A further reading will reveal a string of first-person pronouns referring to God. "'I will bring you. . . . I will stretch out My hand, . . . I will grant this people'" (Exod. 3:17, 20, 21).

Do you ever sound like Moses? Are you making human excuses for the lack of divine activity? Does your church approach new ideas from the standpoint of what God desires to do or what we can do? *Every human excuse is nothing less than unbelief.* It is our unbelief that is limiting our growth, not our lack of resources.

3. Focusing on supernatural empowering calls the church to prayer

Once we fully realize that church growth is a divine activity accomplished through yielded human vessels, prayer will become the number one priority of the church. But until we understand the supernatural activity of God, prayer will always be a last resort when all of our programs and planning fail. "We did all we could and nothing worked, so we decided to pray." Unfortunately, that is precisely the strategy of many Christians and many churches. Prayer meetings are given little weight by the average church because we attempt few things that are beyond our natural ability.

The lack of dependence on prayer is a clear indication of our lack of understanding of the nature and character of God. When we come to understand that we are totally dependent and that God is omnipotent, our first priority will be to pray. When a church takes seriously the demand of the Great Commission, it will realize that it cannot faithfully fulfill its purpose statement without divine empowering.

Every stage of the design and implementation process must be bathed in prayer. God's design will always be more effective than our own, and the only way to know His design is through prayer.

4. Focusing on supernatural empowering ensures that God receives the glory

Paul prayed that the believers in Ephesus would experience supernatural empowering, sense an assurance of Christ's indwelling presence, and receive an understanding of the love of Christ so that they would be filled up to the fullness of God (Eph. 3:14–21). Paul prayed that believers would become all they were intended to be so that the church would become all God designed it to be. What was the church designed to be? *Nothing less than the full expression of God Himself* (Eph. 1:22–23). The crucifixion, resurrection, and exaltation of Christ was on behalf of the church so that we might reveal God fully to the world. In the same manner that Jesus was the full revelation of God while on earth, the church is to reveal God fully (Eph. 3:10). When this occurs, God will receive the glory.

Look at the ending of Paul's prayer: "Now to Him who is able to do exceeding abundantly beyond all that we ask or think, according to the power that works within us, to Him be the glory in the church and in Christ Jesus to all generations forever and ever. Amen" (Eph. 3:20–21). When the church fulfills its mission through supernatural empowering, God receives the glory. He will receive the glory because everyone will know that what has been accomplished was clearly beyond the resources and ability of the people of the church.

Keep the Focus on Obedience to the Great Commission

Church growth is not our goal; obedience to the Great Commission is our goal. When we are obedient to the Great Commission, church growth will be the natural result. This understanding will ensure that the church's focus and motivation are always the proper ones.

It is easy to emphasize church growth for the wrong reasons. Growth could become an issue of pride. Leaders may be lured by desire to be recognized as a church growth leader at the local, state, or national level, but that is not a legitimate or sustaining force for church growth. When numerical growth is tied to "nickels and noses," people will lose interest. You will hear people complain that the church or pastor is not interested in meeting needs. Church members will begin to see the church as focused on numbers and not ministry. We should begin by examining our own motives. If our motives our right, then we should communicate those motives.

There is only one proper motivation—*obedience to the Great Commission.* Keeping this the focus of our church will help us to maintain a high level of spiritual integrity. Such integrity will be the greatest incentive for lay involvement. Born-again believers who are walking in the Spirit want to see their churches faithfully fulfill the Great Commission. When opposition arises to a Great Commission strategy, the believers will be able to see it for what it is—carnal disobedience. People may mount a convincing opposition to an emphasis on numerical church growth by questioning motives, but they cannot oppose obedience to the Great Commission without revealing their own disobedience. A Great Commission focus can be the impetus for revival in the church.

The church that concentrates on the Great Commission will:

• Keep the focus biblical and spiritual

• Ensure the church of supernatural empowering

• Provide a balanced strategy

• Motivate the laity

• Lead to natural church growth

Create a Great Commission Task Force

It is one thing to state one's desire to be obedient to the Great Commission; it is quite another to take steps to implement a Great Commission strategy in the church. I recommend that every church appoint or elect a Great

Commission Task Force (GCTF). This should be a blue-ribbon task force made up of decision makers with a heart for the Great Commission and an effective prayer life.

Members of the task force

Members can be appointed or elected according to the normal processes of your church. I believe the pastor should chair the task force since he is the growth leader of the church. Some churches may be tempted to assign this task to a previously existing body, such as the deacons, trustees, elders, or church council. This may work in some situations, but often it will not be the best approach because not everyone elected for these positions was chosen because of his or her ability or interest in designing the Great Commission strategy of the church. Moreover, a group such as deacons or the church council probably already has a full job description, and making this group serve as the Great Commission Task Force results in piling one more responsibility on them. To do so tends to dilute the work of the GCTF. Use of an existing group like the church council would require a change in the job description of that group to specify their church growth priority.

Some persons already involved in these other ministries will probably be chosen to serve on the GCTF. They are precisely the kind of people you need since they already have great influence in the church. Sunday School leadership should be well represented on the task force since that is the church's primary tool for fulfilling the Great Commission.

All persons who are elected or appointed should be carefully screened for their spiritual maturity and commitment to the church. Some of the characteristics you should look for in task force members are as follows: above reproach, growing in faith, visionary thinkers, involved in the life of the local church, effective witnesses, critical thinkers, and powerful prayer warriors. Men and women alike should be represented as well as persons from different adult-age groupings. If your church or neighborhood is racially or ethnically mixed, you should reflect that mix on the GCTF. Task force participants should be asked to sign a commitment to regular attendance and participation before being elected to service.

However your church works to elect the members of the task force, they should be presented to the church, given authority to work, and be placed on the prayer list at all times. The church should clearly understand that the work of the GCTF is to design an effective strategy, enabling the church to fulfill the Great Commission.

Size of the task force

How large should the GCTF be? That depends somewhat on the size and makeup of your church. No absolutes exist here except that the task force be large enough to accomplish the assignment and small enough to work efficiently. If you make the task force very large in an attempt to represent every segment of the church, it may become too large to do its work well. I would recommend a membership of seven to fifteen persons. The small number allows the dynamics of small group interaction to be maintained. It is possible that some subgroups of the task force will need to enlist other church members to assist them with their specific projects.

Meeting schedule of the task force

The GCTF should meet whenever it proves to be best in each individual church. It is likely better that the pastor establish the meeting time before electing or appointing members so that task force participants know what is required of them as they pray about serving. If the task force is left to determine its own meeting time, they will waste energy trying to establish a time that suits everyone's schedule.

During the initial study phase the work of the task force will be rather intensive, requiring more than a single monthly meeting. The whole task force may meet only once a month to pray, discuss progress, and engage in dialogue, but the subgroups will need to meet more often to accomplish their work.

After the initial strategy is designed and implementation has begun, monthly meetings will probably be sufficient to monitor progress and make needed adjustments. The smaller church may find quarterly meetings sufficient. The pastor will be the person best qualified to judge how frequently the task force should meet.

Putting the Task Force to Work

The task force should be subdivided into three groups based on the specified strategy of the Great Commission:

- Group 1 will study the evangelistic component of disciple making.
- Group 2 will study the assimilation task.
- Group 3 will study the teaching function of discipleship.

The Great Commission Task Force will conduct its work in four distinct phases:

Phase 1: Discovery

Phase 2: Vision setting

Phase 3: Strategy planning

Phase 4: Implementation

Great Commission Task Force

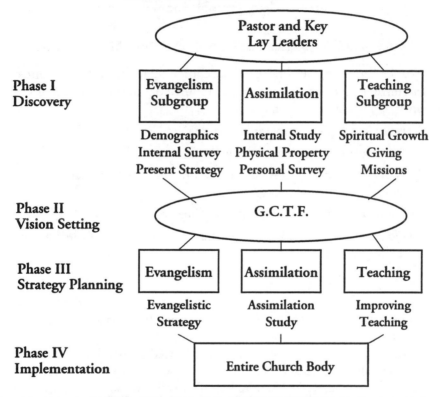

Your task force will be guided by this overarching principle: *Church growth is a supernatural activity accomplished by God through human instrumentation.* For that reason prayer and praise are foundational in empowering the church to fulfill the Great Commission. Thus your entire committee should first assess the strength of your church's worship experience and prayer strategy. You should look at the spirit of the worship service.

You might want to ask these questions:

• Is there a sense of genuine excitement?

• Is the spirit of the people positive, joyous, celebrative, and warm?

- Is the service well planned and executed?
- Do we welcome guests so as to make them feel at home?
- Is the worship service well attended?
- Does our music include a sufficient variety of styles to appeal to all age groups?
- Is the worship center clean, cheerful, and well prepared for Sunday morning?
- Is the sound system such that it enhances the worship experience?

A look at the prayer strategy of the church should help the committee determine the level of commitment the church has to experiencing supernatural empowering. Ask yourselves:

- Is prayer a high priority for our church?
- Are prayer meetings well attended?
- Is prayer a focus of committee, deacon, elder, staff, Sunday School, and other church meetings?
- Do we have an intercessory prayer ministry?
- Do people expect God to empower the church to do that which is naturally impossible?

Phase 1: Discovery

The task force will want to keep prayer and worship at the heart of their discussion and planning in each phase from discovery through implementation.

In Phase 1, the *evangelism subgroup* will need to look both externally and internally. The first concern will be to look at what the church is already doing to reach the community and the effectiveness of its outreach. This study may require that the committee interview leaders of different areas of ministry within the church. What evangelism projects have been conducted in recent years? Be sure to include revivals, special events such as Christmas programs, training for witnessing, Vacation Bible School (with an emphasis on reaching unsaved children and their parents), and other such projects.

A simple survey can be designed to ask how people came to join the church. Statistical information for the last ten years should be collected, studied, and charted. You should determine how many people have joined the church each year. Look at whether those joining are moving their membership from other churches or being won to Christ. Do your evangelism statistics reveal increases or decreases? Chart evangelism growth and transfer growth by age groups. If all the evangelism growth is among children, it means you are doing little more than reaching the children of families in your church. The age-group charts help you evaluate the outreach effectiveness of various ministries.

You should also look at intangible evangelism attitudes. You should ask and honestly answer these questions:

- Is evangelism a priority for our church?
- Do people express a genuine concern for their lost friends?
- Do most members see evangelism as the job of the pastor alone?
- Does our budget reflect an evangelistic priority?
- Do we have an adequate, up-to-date list of persons who are evangelistic prospects?
- Is personal prayer for lost persons a regular feature of various church meetings?
- Does the church have a regular visitation program?
- How many persons are involved in visitation?
- Are members sufficiently enthusiastic about the church to invite their friends?
- Do we have a strategy to make guests feel welcome?
- Do we follow up immediately to contact guests?
- Does the church make good use of publicity?
- Is the building's layout understandable for first-time visitors?
- Do we designate priority parking for guests?

A second part of the study is external, the look outside. What is the makeup of your church field? In other words, who are you trying to reach?

A demographic study will help determine the statistical characteristics of population, such as distribution, density, and vital statistics. It will also include such matters as age, gender, socioeconomic status, religious affiliation, educational background, and the like. You can obtain this information in several different ways. Most denominations now provide demographic information to their churches at little or no expense. You can do your own research by going to city hall or the county courthouse and obtaining the statistical information you desire.

Once you have determined the makeup of your community, you should compare this data with the current makeup of your local church. This should help the church know where to place its greatest emphasis in program and ministry design. For example, if your church membership is predominately senior adult, but the demographic data shows a large influx of young adults with small children, you may need to upgrade the preschool facility; look at the style of music in worship, and develop Sunday School classes or cell groups for young adults in order to be effective in reaching this segment of the population. Any one of these changes could cause objections if not tied to obedience to the Great Commission.

Once the population makeup is determined, someone on this study group might be assigned the task to research the subjective characteristics (psychographics) of each target audience. Books abound on age groups such as Boomers and Busters. The appendix lists a few books that may be helpful to you in studying the characteristics of these different age groups. A word of caution: not all Boomers or Busters fit the stereotypes presented in the books. You would be wise to talk with individuals both in the church and outside the church in each of these categories to see how they feel about certain issues. For example, I brought together a group of Boomers and Busters and asked them, "How do you think we could best reach your friends who are in your age group?" They came up with creative ideas that weren't in any book.

The *assimilation subgroup* is responsible for evaluating the present strategy for assimilating members into the body of Christ. Internal research will reveal how involved the church members are in the life of the church. Here again you need at least ten years of statistical data, unless the church is not yet ten years old. Look at the number of persons actively involved in worship compared to members on the church roll. Compare the attendance in Sunday School or cell groups with worship attendance. How many people are involved in discipling classes and ministry? How many new groups have been started in recent years? Track and chart the number of people who have joined the church with corresponding attendance gains. Are more people joining than attendance averages would indicate? Does the church have a new members' class? What percentage of new members actually attend the classes? Answers to these questions plus the statistical studies and the trend lines will indicates how well the church is assimilating members into the functioning life of the church.

More specific information can be gained by using a churchwide survey that looks at assimilation issues of active and inactive members. Allow your assimilation subgroup to design a survey tool that will help to determine what programs, persons, or events have contributed most positively to assimilation. Some pastors have gone a step further and have interviewed persons who have left the church. They met with them personally and asked why they left and how the church could have better met their needs. This last process demands both courage and tact.

The assimilation subgroup should also look at physical property, acreage, square footage, and parking. Often assimilation is hampered by physical constraints. This is the Water Bucket Theory: If you have a gallon bucket, you can run water in it all day long and still have a gallon of water at the end of the day. The size of the bucket determines how much water it will hold. Your building and property size will impact your ability to reach and assimilate new members.

My rule of thumb is this: Growth plateaus and begins to decline when any portion of the building is 80 percent filled. I call this the Bonsai Effect. The bonsai container ultimately determines the size of the tree. Your committee may find it helpful to read my book, *The Bonsai Theory of Church Growth,* as a part of the discovery phase.[1] It deals with various space constraints.

The *teaching subgroup* will look more at the spiritual dynamics of growth. You will have trouble finding statistics on this, but you should watch for certain clues. One sign of maturity is giving. You should chart total giving as well as per capita giving by members of your church. You should also look at the percentage of the church budget being allocated for mission causes beyond the local church. Does your church exhibit a growing Great Commission mindset? Also look at enrollment and participation in discipleship classes. Finally, you should look closely at leadership. Do you have a growing pool of trained and willing leaders?

Phase 2: Vision setting

In the second phase, the entire task force should reassemble for the exciting work of vision setting. Shared vision ignites a church and propels it forward into supernatural growth. Vision is a clear picture of the church's preferable future, imparted by God to His church, based on a clear understanding of the nature of God, the mission of the church, the needs of the community, and the resources of your church. Since vision originates with God, prayer should saturate this phase of the work of the GCTF.

Each subgroup should be allowed to share their vision for evangelism, assimilation, or teaching. In each case allow members of other subgroups to participate in the discussion and vision setting for each subgroup. Cross-fertilization will generate constructive ideas and encourage the GCTF to work as a team. Do not rush this process. You might want to schedule an overnight retreat for vision setting.

When vision setting, your team must follow these two rules:

1. No one can mention the prohibitive cost of any vision.

2. No one can demean a fellow member's idea.

The next task is to establish a vision statement for the church. A vision statement will help the church define how it can best fulfill the Great Commission in its given setting with its God-given resources. Vision begins with God, is centered in the Great Commission, flows through the core values of the community, addresses community needs, and can be accomplished only by fully using the supernatural resources given by the exalted Lord. We can illustrate vision development with the helpful graphic below.

The mission statement of every church should be the Great Commission. The core values define the essential foundational truths by which ministry must be conducted. The church's essential core values will come from the perfect Word of God. You will not experience authentic growth by violating scriptural principles.

The community needs, as discovered by the various subgroups, should be written out, perhaps on a large board for everyone to see. The resources of the church flow through the gifted members of the church. You can be assured that when God calls the church to a task, He will enable it to accomplish that task. Once you have a clear sense of vision, you should be able to write a simple vision statement.

Notice that our visual has two lines reaching upward from vision to mission. This should remind us that vision must be continually renewed as the church grows. We cannot rely on past vision to energize the church today. This graphic illustration of vision should also tell us that present vision will always have continuity with the past. When you can build present vision on historic vision, the congregation will sense continuity even in the midst of change.[2]

You will know that you have a God-sized vision when it meets the following criteria:

- It originates with God.
- It is centered in and supported by His Word.
- It requires supernatural empowering.
- It is grounded in the Great Commission.
- It leads the church to exalt Christ.
- It requires radical obedience.
- It produces natural growth.
- It demands a willingness to change.
- It requires every church member's best effort.

Phase 3: Strategy planning

Vision setting naturally leads to strategy planning, which is the third phase. The task force should again be broken into the respective subgroups and asked to take the discovery data and the vision statement and begin to develop strategy that will enable the church to accomplish its specific vision, which will, in turn, enable the church to fulfill the Great Commission.

The *evangelism subgroup* should design a strategy for reaching the unsaved community around the church. Such a plan will require that this subgroup address negative attitudes that are a deterrent to outreach. It should look at plans for training laypersons to be involved in witnessing as well as events that might make the unsaved receptive to the witness of members. This group may want to evaluate the attractiveness of the physical plant to visitors. Matters such as parking and signing of the building are important considerations for outreach. This group should also look at changing, establishing, or enhancing the church's image in the community. The church must create visible symbols that say to the community that we are concerned about you and welcome you to our family. The subgroup will inevitably need to address the worship style if it is determined that worship style is a major barrier to reaching the community around the church.

The *assimilation subgroup* will make recommendations for retaining new members and reclaiming old members. Such recommendations will necessarily address attitudes, physical space, and intentional strategy. This group may want to address the reorganization of the Sunday School or the creation of new units to make it easier for newcomers to find acceptance. They should design an intentional strategy for assimilating new members of every age group.

The *teaching subgroup* should make specific recommendations for improving the quality of the entire teaching ministry, including Sunday School, discipleship training, and missions education. Because this subgroup is concerned about spiritual dynamics it should address gift discovery,[3] teacher training, and the total involvement of the body of believers.

Remember, each subgroup should have the freedom to invite other members to participate in the strategy planning as they feel the need. For example, as the teaching group discusses the missions training program, they should invite persons who are teaching missions. In a similar fashion they will want to invite the children's leaders to give input when the children's program is being discussed. This broader involvement will give the task force's work greater credibility and utilize the total resources of the church membership without making the GCTF so large that it cannot function. In general the more people know about the work of the task force, the greater will be their prayer support and their willingness to implement the plans.

Each subgroup should bring their plans in written form with specific goals and dates for accomplishment. If the task force does not tie strategy to specific, observable, and measurable goals, it is unlikely that positive momentum will be generated.

Chapters 6, 7, and 8 will give specific suggestions for developing a strategy for evangelism, assimilation, and teaching. The subgroups should study these chapters as they establish strategy.

A word of caution! Don't copy the specific strategy of this book, any other book, or church. Your Great Commission strategy will need to be customized and contextualized to meet the specific needs of your community and based on the resources available to your church. You can do it!

God has promised the resources. No one knows better how to design a growth strategy for your specific situation than you and those God has placed in your local church according to His sovereign design (1 Cor. 12:18). You are the growth expert.

Phase 4: Implementation

The fourth and final phase is implementation. The GCTF should come back together to consider the overall strategy for fulfilling the Great Commission. A document that outlines the strategy should be prepared and presented to the church for approval and implementation.

If you have done your work well, this will be a time of celebration and churchwide dreaming. Now the entire church can share the joy of watching God work through the strategy He has given to grow His church naturally and supernaturally.

After the plan is approved, the task force should meet as needed (not less than quarterly) to evaluate and modify the strategy and monitor progress. Be flexible and open to change as God guides.

Create a Positive Climate for Change

The most difficult component of church growth for many longtime church members is the prospect of change. In our constantly changing world, people are looking for stability. This prospect of change is threatening, especially in the church. We hear it in the oft-repeated refrains, "I like things the way they are," or "We've never done it that way before." Church growth leaders are challenged to turn change into a positive experience.

We all agree that change is inevitable. We are all changing in many ways every day. We are maturing, both physically and spiritually. The physical changes are more noticeable as waistlines sag, hair falls out, and wrinkles appear overnight. Spiritually we are being changed from glory into glory into His image.

Our world is changing. Our family structure is changing. Babies are born and family members die. Whether we notice it or not, our church has changed, is changing, and will change. It changes as the members grow older. It changes as new members are added or old ones leave or die. We cannot stop the change; we can only channel it toward effective Great Commission strategy.

As we institute intentional changes they should never be capricious. Change for change's sake has no motivational basis. A recent article in a local newspaper quoted one pastor who called himself "an evangelist for change." I think I understand what he was saying, but his attitude may seem cavalier when one is dealing with the church of the living Lord Jesus. Many value the church as the rock of stability in an ever-changing world. We must not change the biblical essence of the church. We must not change the immutable message of the cross. But we must either change the outward essence of the church or fail to effectively fulfill the Great Commission in our day. Subtle change is already occurring in the church, but an intentional Great Commission strategy will often require intentional and visible change.

Richard Beckhard, in his recent book *Changing the Essence,* argues that certain conditions must exist to create the proper atmosphere for changing the essence of an organization. While Beckhard is primarily addressing the business community, we can learn from his suggestions.

1. Why do we exist? Change must occur when there has been a change in the mission of an organization.

2. How do others perceive us? A change in identity will necessitate organizational change.

3. Why do they belong? Stockholder relationships will often necessitate intentional change.

4. How do we get work done? Changes in technology and the marketplace force us to look at operations.

5. What do people value and expect? Changes in culture will ultimately affect every organization.[4]

We can apply Beckhard's questions to the church. Let's look at them one at a time.

1. Why do we exist?

We might argue, correctly I think, that we cannot change our mission statement. We are steadfastly bound to the Great Commission. Yet many churches have already changed in such a way that they no longer fulfill that original and God-given purpose statement. Many have lost the vision for reaching their community. The church was planted with that vision, it flourished in the past because of that vision, but now it has settled into a comfortable maintenance mode where fellowship issues often outweigh concern for the lost. In this case, changing the design will require that the church renew its commitment to its God-given mission statement. *This is the most fundamental change issue in church growth.*

2. How do others perceive us?

Perceptions are always changing. At one time your church may have been viewed as thriving, young, and aggressive. Now it may be seen as a stable, older, hard-to-penetrate community. A turbulent history may have created unkind perceptions of your church. Your building and grounds create perception. You may argue that some of the perceptions are not accurate. That is a moot point! Perception is often more powerful than reality. The church must continually work to ensure that the perception of the church in the community enables it to fulfill the Great Commission. Fundamental changes in structure, organization, operations, and/or facilities may need to be considered to change a negative community perception.

3. Why do people belong?

Every church is constantly going through change in stockholder relationships. The church's stockholders are the present and potential members. On a continuous cycle, people get involved, become disillusioned, and drop out. Some of the material your committee has collected should tell you why people belong, or for that matter, why they feel that they no longer belong. The plateaued or declining church must change in a positive manner at this point or ultimately die.

4. How do we get work done?

Technological advances have changed and will continue to change the way we get our work done. The church would be foolish to ignore the advantages modern technology has brought to the workplace. Computers, fax machines, and telecommunications advances should enable us to more effectively minister to our constituency. Be warned, however, that technological advances will never replace the need for intimate and personal caring. The church must welcome changes that will enable it to accomplish its task more efficiently, while at the same time remaining confident of its supernatural empowering.

5. What do people value and expect?

The expectations and values of people have certainly changed, and the church that does not understand and relate to these changes will not advance kingdom work. Your understanding of the needs and values of different age groups will better enable you to apply the healing power of the gospel where the pain exists. For example, knowing that Boomers are concerned about their children may help to design an effective outreach strategy for reaching the Boomer. Understanding that senior adults are often forced to deal with issues of loneliness and grief will enable the caring church to better reach and minister to this age group. To touch lives we need to know what is happening in the changing lives of people.

Here caution and balance are needed. Some churches in their desire to accommodate cultural changes have compromised on core values—the biblical distinctives of the church. In our consumer-oriented society and market-driven age we must always bear in mind that the gospel alone is eternally relevant and that this present age is passing away. We cannot allow the church to be squeezed into a cultural mold, but we must allow the Holy Spirit to transform the church, and through the church, the world.

Those who appeal to the world on their own terms may draw large numbers to a market-driven, consumer-pleasing community, but they will not grow the church. The attempt to build the "Church Lite," focused on felt need, soft on commitment, and devoid of the message of the cross may be a popular fad, but such compromise will only weaken the church. *We must be Spirit led, not market driven.* The Holy Spirit knows more about the ultimate needs of people than they know themselves. Thus the Spirit-led church will meet not just felt needs but real needs. The church must please God, not the consumer, if we are to experience supernatural empowering. Church Lite will never work in a sin-heavy world.

If your GCTF has done its work well, you already have many of the elements necessary to create momentum for positive change. Link all change to the mission of the church; it is the only compelling reason for the church to change. Here are a few helpful suggestions to enable the church to overcome the natural resistance to change.

1. Anchor change to the heritage of the *past*. Review the many changes we've already made to fulfill the Great Commission.

2. Tie it to the *present*. We are in the process of change. Is our present change productive or nonproductive?

3. Project it into the *future*. By the grace of God, here is what the church can be.

4. Expect God to work supernaturally. We fear change because we prefer the security of the status quo over the uncertainty of the future. If your vision comes from God, you can relax in the assurance that He knows and controls the future. Change must always be undergirded by prayer and Bible study.

5. Give biblical examples and principles of change. The Bible is full of stories in which obedience mandated change.

6. Point to some positive role models. These models can be members of your church who have led in change or a sister church that has had a good experience with planned change. You should also use biblical examples of persons who were change agents.

7. Build strong community relationships. Relationships are the glue that keeps the church together while change occurs.

8. Don't force change, implement it.

9. Give the people the facts. Informed, Spirit-led people will make the right decisions.

10. Don't give up at the first sign of opposition. Change will offend some people. Some folk are like the old-timer who was asked by a visitor, "You must have seen a lot of changes in your day?" "Yes sir," he replied. "And I voted against every one of them."

11. Allow sufficient time so that change is evolutionary rather than revolutionary.

12. Invite those most affected by the change to share input and verbalize their feelings.

13. Expect some confusion and be willing to make alterations on negotiable matters.

14. Keep casting the vision and allow the Holy Spirit to work.

15. Start with those who are willing to grasp the future. In some instances it might be wiser to leave some of the traditional structure and add to it.

16. Keep your language and attitude positive.

Conclusions

If you are tempted to skip the design phase and move on to more important issues of organizing and building, don't! The design phase may appear to be a waste of valuable time to the action-oriented people of the church, but it will pay rich dividends. It will ultimately save energy, resources, time, and relationships. It will help you to avoid false starts, confusion, and hurt feelings. You can't build an effective church without a good set of blue-prints. Take the time to draw the plans, and the building process will go more quickly and smoothly.

Make sure that you take seriously the focus on the supernatural empowering during the design phase, or you will continually be frustrated by the lack of vision and faith that will plague the planning process. If you have ever been involved in a sterile, long-range planning process that is devoid of supernatural thinking, you understand what I mean.

Remember that every design decision must be inextricably bound to the mandate of the Great Commission. Will this plan enable the church to fulfill the Great Commission? A Great Commission mindset will ensure proper motivation and supernatural empowering. With these prin-ciples in mind we will now look at the overall organization of the small-group Bible-study program of the church.

Organizing the Bible Study Program

*T*he term organizing is about as exciting to most of us as a rubdown with steel wool. It doesn't excite us the way sharing vision or reaching the lost does. Most church growth practitioners do administration out of necessity, not out of desire. Nevertheless, a good organizational strategy is as critical to church growth as any other component. Without it much of the hard work that goes into outreach, assimilation, and teaching will be dissipated. This chapter will look at the options available for organizing your Bible study program.

The Biblical Pattern

I realize that it may be hard to sell you on the value of organizing for growth, so it may be helpful for us to begin with several biblical examples.

Moses' example

Moses had led Israel from Egyptian bondage. He had withstood the challenges of the Pharaoh's magicians and had secured safe passage for God's chosen people. When Pharaoh recovered and sent his armies to retrieve his work force, Moses had held aloft the rod as God parted the Red Sea for Israel and then in turn destroyed the Egyptians with the collapse of the walls of water. Through Moses' leadership God had provided water and food for the traveling horde. Victory over the brutal Amalekites had prompted Israel to build an altar to the Lord.

All appeared to be going well. The slaves had been freed. God had met their every need. Victory had been assured by the hand of the Lord. Moses must have felt like the pastor who has just turned around the declining church. The people had a future and a vision. Moses' relatives had heard about the good fortune of Israel, and his father-in-law, Jethro, the priest of Midian, came to join with the victorious people. Victory tends to draw people like flies to honey. Well, enough of the fun already!

The day after the victory celebration, Moses sat before the people from morning to evening, judging the people (Exod. 18:13). Everyone must have had their own agenda. One complained that his tent was too crowded. Another argued that he had been forced to park his camels too far from the camp. Growth has a way of compounding problems and eliciting complaints.

Jethro questioned Moses, "What is this thing that you are doing for the people? Why do you alone sit as judge and all the people stand about from morning until evening?" (Exod. 18:14). Do you think Moses would have volunteered for this task? I'm confident that Moses would have preferred to go a second round with the Amalekites than sit through one more Sunday School council meeting and judge between the teachers complaining about lack of space, quarterlies, and coffee. From victorious conqueror to Sunday School administrator must have seemed like quite a demotion.

Do you ever feel like all you do is sit around from morning till night dealing with complaints and squabbles—administrative details? Who knows, the people of Israel could have been arguing about the mysterious disappearance of Sunday School supplies. "I bought those scissors with my own money. Why do you think I locked them in the closet?" I am convinced that Sunday School teachers have single-handedly kept the Scalage lock people in business. We must lock up our pencils, crayons, paper, coffee, quarterlies, and other Sunday School essentials lest they mysteriously disappear. I wonder if Moses had to deal with the allocation of Sunday School space to meet the needs of the growing tribes? "Give up our room for that singles class! You must be kidding! We have just finished decorating it. We spent our own money buying those drapes. Who do you think put the carpet on the floor and the pictures on the wall?"

Moses had a problem. No, to be precise, Moses *was* the problem. He was a strong, visionary leader, but a poor administrator. He was trying to do all the administrative work alone. He had failed to organize Israel so that the work could be easily accomplished. Perhaps he had a tinge of a messiah complex, thinking that the work couldn't be done unless he did it. Look at Moses' answer to Jethro's question: "Because the people come to me to inquire of God" (Exod. 18:15). He explained that he had to judge between a man and his neighbor and make known the statutes of God. Do you ever feel like you're being called on to play God?

Did Moses get a pat on the back and a word of sympathy from his father-in-law for working so hard? No! Listen to what Jethro said: "The thing that you are doing is not good. You will surely wear out, both yourself and these people who are with you, for the task is too heavy for you; you cannot do it alone" (Exod. 18:17–18). Jethro gave Moses great advice. You should teach the people the law of God, then select able men of integrity who fear God and place them as leaders of thousands, of hundreds, of fifties, and of tens. These men can bear the burden with you and the people will go to their place in peace. Moses listened to his father-in-law and organized Israel so the needs of everyone could be met.

Jethro's organizational principles are still relevant. Every growing church must find some method for breaking down ministry responsibility and supervision into manageable portions. Without an adequate organizational plan, the growing church will first stagnate and then begin to decline.

Most persons who write in the church growth field give attention to various *growth barriers.* Most agree that one of the first growth hurdles occurs when a church reaches an attendance figure of 100–150. One of the factors that can cause a church to stop growing at this size is organizational complexity. If the church has organized small groups for Bible study and the average size is 10–15 persons, they will now have 8–15 small groups. That number of groups cannot be adequately administrated by any one individual. Thus the small groups must be reorganized so that administration is accomplished through several individuals.

New Testament examples

Jesus and His disciples faced a seemingly insurmountable problem— feed a large crowd with five loaves and two fish. The great multitude had followed Jesus into a desolate place and had listened to Him teach throughout the day. The disciples, observing the lateness of the hour, suggested that Jesus dismiss the crowd so they could scatter throughout the surrounding countryside and villages and buy food. Jesus instructed the disciples to feed the hungry crowd. The disciples complained about the cost and effort of such a plan (Mark 6:37). (Some things never change!)

Jesus first instructed His disciples to find out what resources were available. They had failed to take into account the inexhaustible resources of the Lord. We, too, are frequently guilty of underestimating the resources available to the growing church.

I wonder, however, if the disciples were not more concerned by the logistics involved in feeding five thousand hungry persons than the availability of the resources? Jesus commanded the hungry people to recline by groups of hundreds and fifties (Mark 6:39–40). Jesus had a simple organizational strategy—break the large number of hungry people into manageable groups so that they could be fed by His followers.

This is precisely what organizing the church for growth is all about. If the church is going to fulfill the Great Commission by reaching the unsaved, assimilating the saved into the body, and teaching all believers to obey the commands of Christ, it must be organized to do so in an efficient manner.

One last biblical example bears a quick glance. The Jerusalem church was experiencing dramatic growth as the number of disciples was increasingly daily (Acts 6:1). The rapid growth created some natural growth challenges. The Hellenistic Jews believed their widows were being neglected in the daily serving of food. They believed the native Hebrews were showing partiality to their own widows. They complained! Sound familiar? Growth will create problems, particularly if the organizational strategy does not keep pace with the growing needs of the people.

The twelve had a plan. They asked the congregation to select from their number men of good reputation whom they could put in charge of this task. The apostles understood that they could not adequately minister the Word if they neglected prayer and teaching (Acts 6:4). Thus the apostles expanded the organization and delegated the pastoral care of the widows to the seven men elected by the congregation.

The result of their strategy was continued growth: "And the word of God kept on spreading; and the number of the disciples continued to increase greatly in Jerusalem, and a great many of the priests were becoming obedient to the faith" (Acts 6:7).

This passage marks a critical juncture in the life of the Jerusalem church. The complaints, had they not been addressed, could have led to dissension and hindered the church in fulfilling the Great Commission.

The answer to the growth problem was not to cease reaching out, but rather to develop an organizational strategy to meet the total needs of the people without overtaxing a few leaders.

Many churches experience a growth spurt and the accompanying growth pains, and they back away because they expect the pastor or a few key leaders to solve all the problems and do all the work. This reduces their church's growth momentum and renders them ineffective in fulfilling the Great Commission. A simple but flexible and comprehensive organizational strategy is a must to maintain the positive growth momentum given by the Spirit.

The Need for an Organizational Strategy

I cannot overemphasize the importance of an organizational plan to ensure effective and balanced growth. In talking with pastors, staff persons, and other lay leaders, I often detect their lack of concern about organizational issues. Some seem to feel that organization would actually thwart the movement of the Spirit. While it is true that we can make an idol of any organizational plan, it is also true that God always works to bring order out of chaos. Paul reminded the enthusiastic Corinthians that God was not a God of confusion, but one of peace and harmony (1 Cor. 14:33). *An effective organizational plan simply places the resources of the church at the full disposal of the Lord, that they might be used in the most efficient manner for the fulfillment of the Great Commission.*

A good organizational strategy will have seven positive effects on your church.

Positive Effect 1: A good organizational strategy will enable your church to faithfully fulfill the Great Commission. Our concern is not to grow the church but to obey the Great Commission. God has promised to empower His church to fulfill the Great Commission. It is God who desires to grow His church. Our role is to put all our resources at His disposal in the most efficient manner possible. The church at Jerusalem would have been a less-effective tool if it had not developed a strategy for meeting the needs of the Hellenistic widows. Our response to the Great Commission demands that we have a good organizational strategy.

Positive Effect 2: A good organizational strategy will serve as a master plan and thus help avoid costly missteps. As I work with growing churches to help them meet the space needs caused by growth, I always emphasize the need for a master plan. A master plan enables you to plan ahead, thus avoiding costly mistakes that will make your building or property less useful. Without a master plan, churches often waste land or build facilities that are less than efficient. In a similar way, a good organizational strategy should function like a master plan in allocating people and resources to fulfill the Great Commission.

Positive Effect 3: A good organizational strategy will enable your church to manage its resources. While God's resources are unlimited, most churches face several resource issues that, if not managed well, can inhibit the growth of the church. The primary resources are people, money, land, and building space. I firmly believe that God always provides an abundance of resources in all these areas, but He requires that we be good stewards. For example, the laity of the church have a limited number of hours they can give to volunteer service. If we spend hours in nonproductive committee meetings, we may lack time to visit the lost or call class members.

An organizational plan will enable you to determine which activities best enable the church to fulfill the Great Commission and therefore allocate its resources wisely. Such a strategy will also protect the leaders from being accused of being unfair or bowing to special-interest groups.

The apostles could have felt the pressure of the Hellenistic Jews and responded by spending their time serving tables. Such a strategy, while it may have placated the demands of a few, would have been a poor use of the time of the apostles. A plan helps the church respond properly and adequately to the needs of the church with the resources of the Lord.

Positive Effect 4: A good organizational strategy for the whole Sunday School will create a team spirit. One of the deadliest diseases that can infect the growing church is "turfism." Turfism causes the afflicted individuals to focus on their own needs or programs with little concern for the total mission of the church. This disease can infect church staff persons as well as laity. It also appears to be communicable and spreads rapidly.

The Sunday School must be staffed with persons who place the needs of the church above their own needs. Otherwise they will attempt to build their class or department with little regard to the needs of others, demanding their rights, refusing to cooperate when asked to create a new unit or to promote members. Such strongholds of authority can negatively impact the work of the entire Sunday School. Although an organizational strategy will not immediately eradicate turfism, it will in time help to control and finally eliminate it. The organizational strategy keeps the focus on the mission and the good of the whole, thus creating a team spirit.

Positive Effect 5: A good organizational strategy for the Sunday School will provide for better communication. As the church grows, communication becomes increasingly difficult. The larger the number of people, the greater the possibility for misunderstanding. By organizing the Sunday School into small groups, communication is brought down to a more personal level.

Positive Effect 6: A good organizational strategy that includes the whole Sunday School program will help you create new units. Church growth authors universally agree that the key to growth is the creation of new units. These new units broaden the base of the pyramid, enabling it to sustain greater height. New units tend to grow more quickly than older, established units. However, the creation of new units causes crises in some churches. Accusations are heard ranging from "They're splitting our class" to "They're stealing our members." An organizational plan will enable you to start new units where you need them most and to relate their creation to the church's overall strategy.

Positive Effect 7: A good organizational strategy enhances the total ministry of the church. A comprehensive plan allows the small parts to be seen in the context of the whole and thus ensures that the church has a balanced and integrated ministry. Without such a plan it is easy for the church's ministry to become unbalanced. It could, for example, provide space for new preschool classes without taking into consideration where to put the parents of these preschoolers. Or in another case, the church could emphasize evangelism but ignore assimilation and discipleship. Such an unbalanced emphasis could result in many conversions without greatly increasing Bible study attendance.

Organization Based on the Sunday School

The Sunday School has proven to be an effective means for organizing the church. It is simple, flexible, and comprehensive.

Simple

Every church must have some method for organizing its people for Bible study. This requires every church to maintain a Bible teaching organization involving all age groups. A church must decide whether to build on the strength of the Bible teaching program or to create some other organizational strategy. For many church members the small Bible study group is their most natural connection to the life of the church. As the church grows, people may be attracted through the exciting worship service, but they will be assimilated through small-group interaction. Thus the organizational strategy based on these small groups has a preestablished trust relationship. The simplicity of organizing through the Sunday School makes it a natural choice for churches of all sizes.

Flexible

The Sunday School organization has infinite flexibility and can grow with the church. Thus you will not be faced with developing a totally new organizational strategy at each phase of church growth. A Sunday School based on age-graded groupings can be easily reorganized at each level of growth. This flexibility is not found with other organizational plans.

Comprehensive

Organizing through the Sunday School embraces the full scope of the Great Commission and involves every age group in your church. The organizational plan through Sunday School is so comprehensive that many churches have found this an effective way to organize their professional staff as the church grows.

When I first went to Norfolk, I had one staff person other than myself. He was involved in music ministry. The next staff position I added was in preschool, then discipleship. In truth I was adding people haphazardly based on what I couldn't do, rather than adding them according to any clear operating plan. As we continued to grow, it became clear that the Sunday School program of our church involved the greatest number of people and provided the obvious organizing principle. Thus I developed a simple staff plan based on the desire to fulfill the Great Commission through the Sunday School. Early in our growth, the plan included a minister of worship and a minister of education. Because of my special interest in the Sunday School program, I had a dual role as pastor and minister of education for eight years. My first staff organization could be illustrated like this:

Since the Sunday School involved the greatest number of people, I began to develop ministry positions for the various age groups. As the

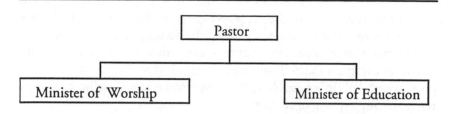

church grew in complexity, I added an administrator to look over financial affairs, the office work, and the building. We finally added a position related to pastoral care and counseling. The later and more complex staff plan might be illustrated as follows:

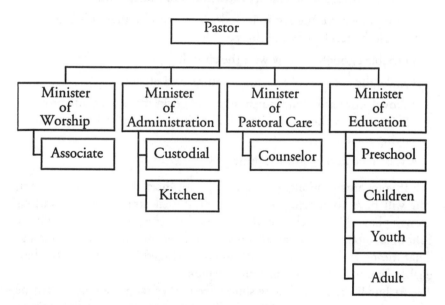

Notice that the larger staff plan simply expanded on the organizational strategy of the church. This is not the only way to organize the large staff, but it is a simple method that grows naturally with the Sunday School and thus the church.

Organizing the Bible Study

When you set up your Sunday School organization or cell group structure, you will begin to choose a system for organizing adult classes. This critical choice will determine your strategy for creating new units, which is at the heart of expanding the Bible-teaching ministry of church growth.

Arthur Flake, one of the early architects of the evangelistic Sunday School, wrote: "The question of grading the Sunday school is an old one. It is in many respects the most important question which confronts Sunday school workers today. The reason for this is that if a Sunday school is properly graded, it is possible to have everything else of value needed to make the Sunday school efficient."[1]

Criteria for your organizational principle

Every Bible study program needs an organizational principle that meets some basic criteria:

- Simple enough for members and visitors to understand
- Comprehensive enough to include everyone who presently attends or should be reached by the church
- Flexible enough to grow with the church
- Make the creation of new units natural and obvious
- Provide for natural movement of members in the Bible study program to counteract the gravitational pull of introversion and the accompanying stagnancy
- Maximize known growth principles

If your organizational principle does not meet the first three criteria, you will have to develop a new organizational strategy at the various growth phases of your church. Remember this: The purpose of the Sunday School or Bible study organization should determine the basis of grading. That means your Sunday School should be graded in a manner that best enables you to fulfill your mission statement.

Arthur Flake asked, "Why should we bother with grading?" Then he answered his own question: "It makes it easier to reach those who ought to be in the Sunday school."[2]

J. N. Barnette also based his rationale for grading on the purpose statement, but he defined it a bit differently: "A Sunday school exists for the purpose of helping to meet the spiritual needs of individuals. Therefore, each individual should be placed in a Sunday school so as to secure the greatest spiritual benefit."[3]

"Nothing precedes purpose," insists Rick Warren. "The starting point for every church should be the question, 'Why do we exist?' Until you know what your church exists for, you have no foundation, no motivation, and no direction for ministry."[4]

I have suggested that you should build your Sunday School and your church on the Great Commission purpose statement. In that case you should seek a grading system that will best enable you to accomplish the threefold task of making disciples—going, assimilating, and teaching.

What are your options for grading?

Grading the preschool through college divisions in the Bible study program is pretty much standardized by the secular educational system and the size of the Sunday School. Preschool groups itself naturally into infants, ones, twos, threes, fours, and fives. The smaller school may need to adapt the grading scheme to match both the space available and the number of children attending the Sunday School. For example, you could group infants with ones, twos with threes, and fours with fives. The larger church, on the other hand, may need several classes of one-year-olds.

Most churches prefer to divide school-age children accord to the pattern of the local school system. For example, if grades seven through nine are together in a central junior high, your Sunday School should put these age groups into the same class, or department in the case of the larger Sunday School. If the local school system has only grades seven and eight together, you would be wise to follow that same grading system since the young people will have established relationships at school that can carry over into the Sunday School. The children and youth will want to be grouped with their peers. The smaller school may need to combine two or three grades to have enough children to have a strong class. As your school grows, simply divide by school grades. The larger school in turn may have several second-grade classes.

Grading the adults in the Bible study program has been a greater challenge for many churches. Some adults appear to have an aversion to revealing their true age. I have jokingly suggested that there are only two options for the grading of adults—age or weight. I suspect that if you threatened to grade based on weight, you might find a greater receptivity for age grading. Even though many pastors, educators, and lay leaders grimace when you mention grading adults, it is essential that some system be used or the Bible study organization will stagnate and become ineffective for either outreach or assimilation. The stagnant Sunday School will often focus on fellowship and Bible study, but it will generally be less than effective in these areas than the aggressively growing school.

Let's look at several options for grading adults as we keep in mind the six criteria by which we should evaluate our organizational strategy.

Option 1: Grading the Sunday School based on scholastic attainment. This system works well up through the college department, but it breaks down in the adult division. It becomes difficult to enforce and does not allow for enough adult divisions to grow the Sunday School. Do we group all those with post-baccalaureate degrees together? I think you can see the problems such a strategy would create.

Option 2: Grading the Sunday School based on social relationships or congeniality. Few educators advocate this strategy since it often leads to cliquishness. I have, however, had people in our church advocate such a strategy. In truth, when the Sunday School is left to its own devices, it will quickly stagnate into pools of congeniality. This plan, if adopted intentionally or by default, will work in opposition to all six growth criteria for an organizational strategy.

Option 3: Grading the Sunday School based on geography. Geography as a grading mechanism has been used by some proponents of cell groups. If the cell groups are established with clear guidelines concerning the development of new cells in a geographic area, this system may work. It is less effective as an organizing principle for the Sunday School that meets in a central building. However, First Baptist, Jacksonville, Florida, has combined geographic grading with age grading. Because of the large attendance in Bible Study, they have divided some groups by age and zip code. This is an innovative step enabling them to maintain the integrity of the age-grading system.

Option 4: Grading the Sunday School by topical interest or special need. This system has been used by some churches for years, but it received additional interest when it was discovered that Boomers respond to churches that meet their felt needs. Now that the initial stage of euphoria has passed, many churches have found this to be ineffective for the overall grading of the Bible study program. It has several inherent weaknesses:

- Interest- or need-based groups often become personality focused. The biggest crowd of adults will be most interested in the topic being taught by their favorite teacher.

- Interest- or need-based groups require constant reorganization. Topics must be changed regularly, usually each quarter. This is time consuming for most staff persons and key lay leaders.

- Interest- or need-based groups find it harder and harder to find new and interesting topics as time passes and the church grows.

- Interest- or need-based groups lack continuity. Because the groups change with the change of topics, this method makes it hard to build relationships and ministry opportunities in small groups.

- Interest- or need-based groups can stifle evangelistic opportunity. It is hard to penetrate these groups once they have been underway for several weeks. The newcomer feels left out.

- Interest- or need-based groups are difficult to explain to members and visitors. Explaining them becomes increasingly difficult as the church increases in size. It has not proven to be an effective strategy for organizing the entire Bible study program.

Many churches have had good success with need-based groups as entry points into the church. Some churches have support groups for divorced or separated individuals, children of alcoholics, and so forth. Churches that have been most successful with such classes have had some termination point for each group, with the intention of having a sense of closure. Their goal is to integrate each person into the mainstream Bible study structure of the church. My own experience has shown that interest- or need-based groups work better on Sunday night or on a weeknight than on Sunday morning; the evening groups have greater flexibility because there is more time for ministry and discussion.

If you want to attempt to use either the need-based or topic-based group as an entry-level group, I suggest that your teacher be a team player who understands the evangelistic purpose of the group, that a specific time period be established for the group, and that every attempt be made to incorporate these persons in the ongoing Bible study program.

Option 5: Grading the Sunday School based on spiritual maturity. I include this option only because I occasionally encounter laypersons who want to argue for such a system. Those making the most vocal arguments are often opposed to reaching new people and also assume that they themselves would be in the most mature spiritual grouping.

The obvious dilemma with this suggestion is that someone must be the judge of spirituality and must set the criteria for advancement. I have not seen any churches that have successfully graded based on spiritual attainment. If someone could devise such a system, it would be a serious deterrent to evangelistic outreach through the small groups since the material being presented in the classroom of more mature believers would be too advanced for the new Christian. This would discourage class members from bringing their unsaved friends to Sunday School.

Option 6: Grading the Sunday School by age. This is a natural method and the standard of Sunday School work. My conviction about the strength of age grading the Sunday school came from experience. I became the pastor of two churches that had age grading through high school but had allowed the adults to stagnate into groups of congeniality. I attempted several grading methods such as topic, need, and spiritual maturity before returning to age grading, the standard of Sunday School work. I had to be convinced to resurrect the dinosaur of the age-graded Sunday School.

Early church growth authors such as J. N. Barnette gave long lists of advantages to age grading:

> What does grading on the age basis do for a Sunday school? Grading locates responsibility for each period of life. Grading locates neglected spans of life. It prevents temptations for teacher-centered classes. Grading provides congenial groups with like interests. Grading simplifies the teaching task. Grading prevents a static condition in a Sunday school.

> Grading anticipates advancement from one life stage to the next. Grading breaks down imaginary social lines and class distinctions. Grading recognizes the supreme worth of every individual. Grading makes the organization of needed classes easy. Grading accelerates the growth of a Sunday school. It prevents classes from enlisting the easy prospect of all ages and neglecting the needy people.

> Grading provides more evangelistic opportunities. Grading prevents the necessity for new members to choose between classes, which is frequently embarrassing. Grading furnishes places of service in a Sunday school for more adult church members. Grading furnishes fair and equitable distribution of prospects. Grading is democratic. Grading recognizes natural stages of life.

> Grading, when followed sympathetically, has produced good growth and improved the quality of work. Grading has pleased the people when they were consulted and given an opportunity to understand the reasons for it.

> The important question for practical people is: Is it profitable? Will a Sunday school graded from birth through older adults enroll

more people, win more people to Christ, and strengthen a church more than a Sunday school that is not graded?[5]

Why were the early architects of Sunday School so committed to the principle of age grading? Arthur Flake listed three reasons:

1. Age grading "makes it easier to reach those who ought to be in the Sunday school."

2. Age grading "makes it easier to teach those who are in the Sunday school."

3. Age grading "makes some individual definitely responsible for winning each lost pupil to Christ."[6]

Note that two out of Flake's three reasons were related to evangelism. Age grading is the secret to an evangelistic Sunday School.

My own experience convinced me that age grading was the most natural means of organizing the Sunday School.

- Age grading is easy to explain to the first-time attender, thus facilitating evangelism and assimilation.

- Age grading takes advantage of the church growth principles of homogeneity and receptivity.

- Age grading counters stagnation by encouraging class members to develop new relationships.

- Age grading is a natural system already built into our thinking from preschool through senior adults.

- Age grading recognizes that pupils the same age generally have similar spiritual needs. Bible study can be related to the developmental needs of the individual. This discovery helped to convince Joseph Dennis that the age-graded Sunday School is one of the most effective tools for building bridges to Baby Boomers.[7]

- Age grading makes it easy to organize outreach and call for accountability.

- Age grading makes it easy to recognize when the Sunday School is graded.

- Age grading makes the Sunday School easier to reorganize.

The challenges of age grading

I am not suggesting that age grading your Sunday School will be easy. Everything worthwhile will involve both challenges and risks. Age grading the Bible study program requires a team spirit, the classification of each individual by age grouping, an up-to-date record system, and regular promotion of all participants.

If you are in a church that has never been age graded or has not recently been age graded, you may hear some objections from those who want to build a large class for their own gratification. Sometimes persons may argue that they are being coerced and are going to leave the church if they are required to promote. If they leave for this reason, don't fret; they would find another reason to leave if you remove this objection. Here are a few of the objections you may hear.

"Our officers and teachers don't understand why we need to age grade." Since a team spirit is important, it is essential that those involved in the task understand both the *what* and the *why*. This is where transparency, patience, and communication skills will pay great dividends. Explain the value of age grading and keep the purpose of Sunday School at the forefront.

"Our teachers are against age grading because they want to keep their present pupils." They may not state their feelings openly. This challenge is often couched in the language of "fellowship," but it is more often related to their comfort zone. It is important that the Sunday School provide opportunities for fellowship, but age grading will not hurt fellowship. Any organizational plan that allows you to grow a Sunday School will require you to move students and create new units.

"Our pastor or Sunday School director is afraid and would rather leave well enough alone." But a great Bible study program is rarely found at the end of the road of least resistance.

"Annual promotion of adults is just too hard to accomplish." You may find yourself thinking this. But remember, you should never be deterred from doing the right thing simply because it is difficult. Annual promotion is no more difficult than reorganizing geographical cell groups or interest-based groups. You must find some way to create new units and to move adults into natural groupings. Age grading with annual promotion is the best way to achieve this. You can make it a big event by creating new departments, visiting chronic absentees, and celebrating the new Sunday School year.

"We don't have enough teachers" or "We don't have enough rooms." If you take seriously either of these excuses, your Bible study program will stop growing no matter how you organize it. If you do not have enough teachers, you must first improve your prayer strategy (Matt. 9:37), then institute a teacher training program (see chap. 8). The growing church must provide additional space either off campus or on campus, during the regular Bible study hour or at another time.

"People will leave the church if we force them to promote." If you are offering quality Bible study and good fellowship, they won't go anywhere. If someone leaves over the commitment of the church to do whatever is necessary to fulfill the Great commission, you may be better off without them.

"Some of our couples have widely varying ages." This has become a more critical issue in our day and must be addressed. Many churches have simply allowed the couple to attend the class that most closely corresponded to the age of the wife. Another way to accomplish the same result is to grade couples based on the age of their oldest child. Here again the age-grading system must be used with a sensitivity to the unique needs of the people involved.

If you are age grading for the first time, move slowly and patiently. Realize that you are changing well-established traditions. Communicate positively about age grading and promotion with teachers and department directors first. If you can sell the teachers on the concept, they will be able to make it a positive experience for the students. Develop a team spirit and clearly tie the age grading to the mission or purpose statement of the church. I find that when laypeople are treated responsibly and given the *why* as well as the *what,* they will respond with enthusiasm. Nevertheless, you should expect some opposition. A few folk feel called to oppose any new idea.

How do you handle those who refuse to cooperate? My father used to tell me that, when you are clearing a field, some stumps simply aren't worth the effort it takes to remove them. The wise farmer just plows around them. In other words you may have a few people who want to be the exception. Let them make the exception rather than you making it. You cannot coerce adults. If you go ahead with most of the people, time will generally deal with the exceptions. Those individuals who remain in a younger class will ultimately feel out of place and seek their proper class.

If you must make an exception for an entire class, give it the most natural age classification, then start a new class below it and above it when they are needed to reach adults. These new classes will begin to grow and promote persons into the stagnant class, requiring the class members to deal with the issue of new relationships.

Do you believe age grading is the most effective way to grade your Sunday School to fulfill the Great Commission? If so, then build the vision, communicate positively, and refuse to give up. It's worth it to see your Sunday School function in a healthy and positive way.

You may be wondering whether it is possible to combine several grading strategies. This is a legitimate and obvious question. The early architects of Sunday School answered this with a resounding no. Arthur Flake argued that mixing grading methods would immediately result in an ungraded school. He insisted that the relationship between classes and departments would break down unless the whole school was graded.[8]

I agree that mixing grading methods usually slows growth. But some large churches with graded Sunday School programs have added some special classes that are ungraded. Some have introduced an entry-level pastor's class for newcomers. This class is usually ungraded and larger than the average adult class. The objective of the class is to reach people who aren't in Sunday School and then involve them in the mainstream of the Sunday School program.

A few large churches have successfully combined ongoing special-interest classes with the age-graded program. For example, Mrs. Criswell and Zig Ziglar taught large, ungraded classes for years at First Baptist, Dallas. These classes did not replace the need for the graded Sunday School. Such classes should only be started with a clear understanding of their purpose.

Larger churches can better tolerate a diversity of grading methods than can the smaller church. In the large church, these exceptional classes are simply a different entrée on the cafeteria line. The large ungraded class in the small church can become a power structure for opposing the pastor's leadership. If you decide to use several systems for grading your Bible study program, make sure that your goals and purposes are clear and well communicated. Otherwise you may create jealousy and strife within the system.

Allow the Organization to Grow with the Sunday School

One value of organizing the church through the age-graded Sunday School is that the Sunday School grows naturally with the numerical growth of the church. In the smaller church the organizational chart will be relatively simple, thus aiding the bivocational pastor or single staff member to effectively administrate the church. As the church grows, the Sunday School organization can be easily expanded to accommodate the number of people attending.

The first step in organizing through the Sunday School is to develop a departmental structure. This has five advantages:

1. It provides a simple organizational structure that can grow as the church grows.

2. It allows for effective communication.

3. It provides for accountability.

4. It promotes a team spirit.

5. It aids in starting new classes.

The small church would probably need no more than three or four departments: a preschool department, a children department, a youth department, and an adult department. Some smaller churches may find it necessary to combine the children and youth. Here is what the organizational chart would look like:

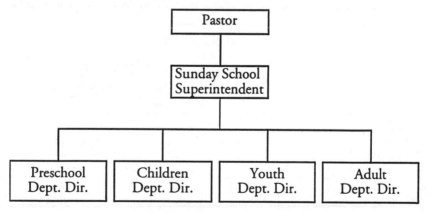

As the church grows larger, the department structure allows for the organization to be easily and naturally expanded. In the charts that follow, I suggest an organizational structure for a medium-sized church and a much larger church. Those titled "minister" may be full-time church staff members while those titled "department directors" may be lay volunteers. Each church can make the organizational chart fit their unique needs.

The average adult department will become visually saturated at about 125 persons. This would mean that the department will be comprised of four or five classes of twenty-five to thirty persons enrolled. If a department

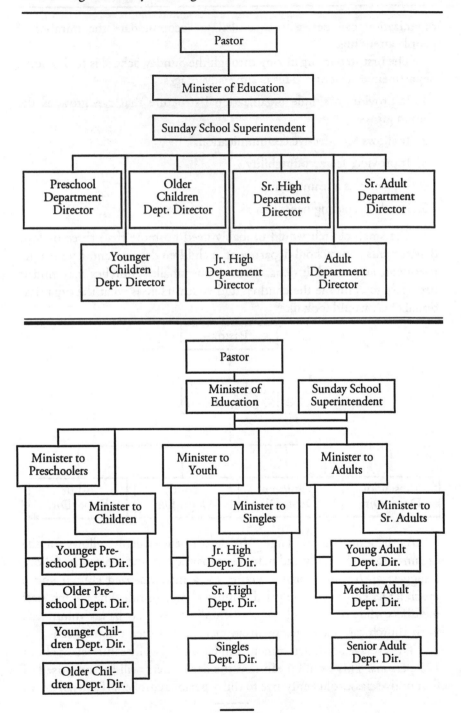

has more than four or five classes, administration becomes more complex and accountability often breaks down If you allow the department to become larger, you must ensure that it is organized into a sufficient number of small groups for adequate caring.

Sunday School or Cells?

Cell groups or Sunday Schools? This choice has created quite a stir in evangelical circles. The recent headline in *Christianity Today* reads, "How Small Groups Are Transforming Our Lives." This shows the interest in cell groups in the evangelical community. The article begins by declaring that 40 percent of Americans participate in small groups and yet we know little about them.[9] In many circles the debate over Sunday School versus cell groups has become intense.

I find this debate amusing because, in truth, the traditional Sunday School accounts for a significant number of the people who are involved in the small-group movement. I have frequently defined a Sunday School class as "a cell group that meets in your church building on Sunday morning" and a cell group as "a Sunday School class that meets outside your building at some other time." Why must we set these in opposition to each other?

I recognize that my definitions are oversimplifications. The cell—or small-group—movement includes many kinds of groups. Charles Arn, editor of *The Growth Report*, lists eight: Bible study, prayer, fellowship, nurture, social, task, accountability, and house church. (See appendix for Arn's chart with descriptions.)[10] It is my conviction that the well-organized Sunday School class can and should accomplish the function of the first seven types of small groups. Not all seven functions will happen during the Sunday morning hour, but the ministry functions can be organized and accomplished through the Sunday School. It may be advantageous to look at the possible advantages of cell groups and Sunday School classes respectively.

Possible advantages of cells

Cell groups cost the church less money than Sunday School because they do not require the church to construct classrooms. This would make cells a good choice for a beginning church or for a church in an area where land is at a premium. Many growing churches that I have visited in countries outside the United States would find the cost of land and building materials for a large Sunday School building prohibitive.

Cells provide more time for prayer and fellowship. Often cells are more relaxed than Sunday School classes because they meet in a home during the week. J. Maroney and Ralph Neighbor argue that the key ingredient of the cell group is the relational aspect, not the cognitive Bible study.[11] The relational aspect of cells is certainly enhanced by the more casual meeting place.

Cells sometimes benefit from the intimacy provided by a home as opposed to a classroom. The use of a home may put the non-Christians at ease. The cell group can thus function as a bridge to fellowship in the larger church.

Many cells have proven to be effective for evangelistic outreach. This requires that the cell group participants be willing to bring their unsaved friends, and the home setting may be less threatening to the non-Christian.

Cells that focus on special or felt needs may be more effective at meeting that special need than a traditional Sunday School class. Sunday School is usually content driven rather than needs driven.

Cells may involve more of their participants in service than the traditional Sunday School class. Maroney and Neighbor argue that this is the most significant difference between the traditional church and the cell-group church. They state that only 10 to 15 percent of the members of the traditional church participate in the ministry, whereas 100 percent of the cell-group members participate.[12] For such a high percentage to be taken seriously, one must assume that participation in the group discussion would qualify as ministry.

Possible advantages of Sunday School

Many of the advantages of the Sunday School strategy can also be presented as criticisms of the cell-group structure. It will be obvious that, if all the variables are the same, I prefer the Sunday School structure to that of cells.

I introduced cells into the structure of First, Norfolk. At one time we had a large number of cell groups functioning in the life of the church. I encountered many of the same difficulties that other pastors across North America have encountered. Those who prefer the cell-group structure for their setting may find these observations about the Sunday School helpful in improving their cell-group ministries.

Sunday School is easier to organize and manage than cells. Anyone who has attempted to get all the records returned from the Sunday School classes can appreciate the difficulty of managing a large Sunday School with numerous classes. This management task is difficult enough when all the classes are meeting in the same building at the same time. The cell-group structure makes the organizational dynamics even more difficult. Cells often meet on different nights of the week in different parts of town. The seemingly simple task of record keeping is made infinitely more difficult with the cells spread across the city. The Sunday School structure allows for closer supervision and greater accountability. For the cell-group structure to work effectively, there must be a high level of commitment by cell-group leaders and close attention paid to supervision and accountability.

Sunday School tends to become less personality centered than cell groups. While any small-group structure runs the risk of having the strong teacher creating a small kingdom, the risk is greatly reduced when the teachers are under the closer supervision possible when the classes meet in the same place and at the same time. The weekly workers meeting can help create a team spirit and monitor class size. A strong leader meeting in a private home often feels less restraint. This can lead to splinter groups.

The Sunday School structure makes it easier to safeguard doctrinal integrity than the cell-group structure. Most Sunday School systems use a standard curriculum for classes. This standardized curriculum, together with the close supervision of the Sunday School, guards doctrinal integrity. Cell groups tend to be more oriented toward relationships than to cognitive Bible study. Maroney and Neighbor note this difference when they indicate that the key ingredient of cell gatherings was the people in the room, not the study material.[13] They note that this is distinctively different from the cell structure of churches in Korea, where the curriculum is extremely detailed. Maroney and Neighbor say that Americans would ignore such detailed instructions.[14]

A recent article in *Christianity Today,* summarizing the findings of Robert Wuthnow, sociology professor at Princeton University, notes that cells "do little to increase the biblical knowledge of their members. Most of them do not assert the value of denominational traditions or pay much attention to the distinctive theological arguments that have identified variants of Christianity or Judaism in the past. Indeed, many of the groups encourage faith to be subjective and pragmatic."[15]

Several years ago I attended a church-growth conference in Fort Worth, Texas, where a cell-group leader was answering questions about cell ministry. The spokesperson criticized the Sunday School model because it required too many trained and qualified leaders. When asked how the cell-group structure handled this same issue, the presenter indicated that their church allowed unbelievers to lead discovery cells because they were based on inductive study questions with no correct answers.

George Barna, church growth pollster, surprised many readers when he suggested that the small-group movement may actually be on the decline. He speculated that the downturn in small-group participation might be accounted for by a tendency toward weak teaching, confusion of purpose, lack of leadership, and such practical concerns as inadequate child care.[16]

The church that finds cells more conducive to its situation must pay careful attention to doctrinal integrity or their cell structure may become little more than a passing fad that may introduce heresy and doctrinal confusion to their church.

The Sunday School structure reinforces the value of the worship service by making attendance more convenient. We are frequently told that Boomers value time more than money. We found that the Sunday School structure allowed us to offer small-group Bible study and a corporate worship experience in a minimum amount of time. The ability to combine both activities on a single morning saved the average couple about ninety minutes each week. It also freed a weeknight. We found that Boomers greatly preferred the convenience of the two events occurring together. We had a very high percentage of Sunday School attenders staying for worship.

Sunday School integrates total family education. The Sunday School structure is designed to enable the entire family to attend Bible study at the same time. This is not only more convenient, it can be utilized by the family to enhance family conversation about the content of the Bible study. The integration of family instruction also solves another major dilemma faced by churches that select the cell structure—child care. We found that cell groups involving young couples with small children dropped off in attendance fairly rapidly, especially during school terms. The expense and difficulty of securing adequate child care soon took its toll on the ability of both the husband and wife to attend the Bible study group on a regular basis.

The Sunday School can be designed to incorporate all the functions of the effective cell group. Robert Logan lists seven key functions of the effective cell: teaching, fellowship, worship, prayer, power, ministry, and evangelism.[17] In the final chapters of this book I will discuss a Sunday School plan that effectively incorporates these facets of small-group ministry. Many criticisms leveled against the Sunday School structure are really directed against large classes using the lecture format.[18] This stereotypical model is not the model used by many growing churches, nor is it the pattern recommended in this book.

Sunday School involves a higher proportion of the church's people than cell groups in a North American setting. Logan argues that the ideal for the cell-group church would be total involvement, yet he discovered a more sobering reality. "This will be a challenging goal for most churches with home Bible-study programs, which usually have less than 25 percent of their attendance involved."[19] If Logan is referring to adult attendance in cell groups, this goal of 25 percent could be compared with 50.9 percent of adults in Southern Baptist churches involved in Sunday School attendance. If we take all age groups through preschool into our formula, Southern Baptist churches average 85.3 percent of their morning worship attendance in small-group Bible study attendance.[20]

In most instances the traditional Sunday School structure will prove to be more effective than the cell-group structure for the church's Bible study program. The cell-group structure may be more effective than the Sunday School structure in some special circumstances: church starts, inner-city churches, churches with inadequate space, and churches in areas where land is prohibitively expensive. Every church will need to determine its own strategy based on its unique context.

Can our church use both cells and Sunday School?

Is it possible to utilize both cell groups and the Sunday school structure? I think it is not only possible but also expedient in the church of the twenty-first century. Many churches have already adopted such a strategy by establishing need-centered cells to meet unique situations, such as parents without partners, Alcoholics Anonymous, and separation and divorce groups. These cells can supplement the traditional Sunday School structure. Many of our Sunday School classes in Norfolk established smaller cell groups that met during the week for prayer or fellowship.

I believe it is possible to use both the cell structure and the traditional Sunday School structure for the organization of Bible study groups. We have often been guilty of forcing everyone to fit into a system we have already devised, such as the age-graded Sunday School that meets only on Sunday morning. While this pattern will work for the vast majority of persons, there are always those who will be an exception to the rule. Why not develop a weeknight or lunchtime Bible study cell group to reach these individuals?

If you plan to use cells and Sunday School for Bible study, I recommend that you use a standard curriculum for both and require the leaders in both cases to be involved in the strategy planning meetings for the Bible study leaders. This will keep everyone on the same playing field, create a sense of team unity, and help guard the doctrinal integrity of the Bible study program. It also simplifies planning, training, and organization. For the participants, it facilitates movement among the groups.

Conclusions

An organizational strategy for small-group Bible study is not only biblical, it is essential for the church that desires to fulfill the Great Commission. An adequate strategy should help the church fulfill its purpose, serve as a master plan, enable the church to manage its resources, create a team spirit, provide for better communication, assist in starting new units, and enhance the total ministry of the church.

The Sunday School can be used as the organization strategy for the church's entire ministry plan. It provides a simple plan that is comprehensive and flexible.

The first step in organizing the Bible study program will be the grading of the Bible study groups. While many options are available, and all have their possible advantages and challenges, age grading is the simplest and most effective method for the growing church for many reasons.

You must decide between a cell structure or the traditional Sunday School structure. In certain situations, such as the new church and the church that is challenged with space or land needs, the cell-group structure may be most advantageous. In the North American church, the cell-group structure creates several challenges that must be addressed. In most churches, the traditional Sunday School structure will prove to be most effective and efficient.

٨

S I X

Designing an Effective Outreach Strategy

*T*he Sunday School that is designed to fulfill the Great Commission must go to work in outreach before anything else. Developing an evangelistic Sunday School and church is not so much a matter of strategy as it is a matter of commitment and climate.[1] The church must first believe that the evangelistic priority is non-negotiable. The church members must have a theological conviction that will empower them to overcome the apathy and fear that paralyzes the average Christian when it comes to outreach. (For a more complete discussion of the theological foundations for creating an evangelistic church, you should read chap. 7 in my book *The Antioch Effect*).

Kirk Hadaway, through his extensive research, has clearly established that the evangelistic zeal of the pastor is the key to the evangelistic success of the growing church. Pastors of growing churches see themselves as more evangelistic than do pastors of plateaued or declining churches. This evangelistic zeal is seen in the participation of the staff in the visitation program of the church. Hadaway discovered that the evangelistic pastor must stress the importance of evangelism, verify its importance by action, and ensure that members are encouraged, trained, and mobilized to visit prospects and witness to friends.[2]

Once the commitment has been made and the climate established, a strategy for discovering prospects, training laity, taking the good news to the community, challenging the lost to commit to Christ, and assimilating and nurturing new believers must be developed. Without an ongoing strategy, evangelistic zeal will be dissipated.

The age-graded Sunday School provides the best organizational structure for organizing the church's outreach program. Every church must tailor the details of its own approach to community outreach because every situation is unique and requires personalized application. While you can learn from the outreach programs of other churches, you need not feel pressure to clone the strategy of any other church. You will need to design your strategy with a clear understanding of your own context and the gifts and resources of your church. Whatever the specific strategy, every church must have an intentional plan and must find some way for organization, evaluation, and motivation.

The material in this chapter will suggest an organizational plan that can be adapted to any size church in any setting.

Historical Precedence

We have history on our side when we choose to utilize our Sunday School as an evangelistic tool. Ann Boylan, who has written the definitive book on the history of the Sunday School movement, documents the unique development of the Sunday School as an evangelistic tool in America. She writes, "Indeed, efforts to use the Sunday School for national evangelization, so important a part of the American story, were wholly absent in nineteenth-century Britain."[3]

Boylan notes that the concern for evangelism in the American Sunday School began to alter the organizational strategy. "In keeping with this goal, Sunday School workers revamped the Schools' organization and program. Small classes, with six to ten pupils per teacher now became the ideal." The practice of rotating teaching staffs was abandoned in favor of assigning a teacher to individual classes on a year-long basis. This allowed the relation between the teacher and students to become more intimate. Teachers also started visiting in the homes of their students to promote the religious progress of the students. The impact was so great that by 1880 the Sunday School had become the primary recruiting ground for church members.[4] Notice that one's purpose will impact organizational strategies.

Chuck Kelley, former director of the Center for Church Growth at New Orleans Baptist Seminary, chronicles the history of evangelism in the

Southern Baptist Convention in his book, *How Did They Do It?* Kelley notes the unique contribution of the Sunday School to the unprecedented evangelistic growth of the denomination. Southern Baptists struggled to embrace Sunday School because of suspicion over its northern heritage and interdenominational roots. Once they had embraced the concept of the Sunday School, they began to focus on its evangelistic potential. J. M. Frost, first secretary of the Sunday School Board, emphasized the grading of the entire school as a key to using the Sunday School for evangelism and growth.

Arthur Flake articulated the growth formula that still serves as the basis of the Southern Baptist Sunday School. Flake's formula is simple but effective:

1. Discover the prospects.
2. Expand the organization.
3. Train the workers.
4. Provide the space.
5. Go get the people.[5]

Southern Baptists have seen a perceptible decline in the rapid growth rate that marked that denomination during the fifties and sixties. Do we thus conclude that the Sunday School is indeed little more than the fossil remains of a once great evangelistic tool? Not so, according to Kirk Hadaway, in his well-researched book on growth principles that work. He notes that many churches allowed the outreach function of the Sunday School to atrophy. When that happened, the supply of new members began to slow, existing classes stagnated, and entire churches became closed fellowships, existing only to serve the needs of their current members. Hadaway discovered that 84 percent of growing churches rated their Sunday School as excellent or good, and 77 percent of growing churches had a regular time for Sunday School visitation.[6] Sunday school still works as a growth tool for those who use it properly.

Leith Anderson, who is often associated with the innovative church movement, argues that those born after 1950 are more likely to enter a new church through something other than Sunday morning worship service. He then suggests something like a church-sponsored Bible study.[7] Sunday School has the potential to be the church growth tool of the twenty-first century.

The Sunday School can be revitalized in your church as an effective growth tool if you will utilize it as such. To do so, start by organizing your outreach program to function through the age-graded Sunday School.

The Advantages of Organizing through the Sunday School

Organizing for outreach through the Sunday School provides the church with clear advantages over alternative methods.

Advantage 1: Organizing through the Sunday School takes maximum advantage of the twin church growth principles of homogeneity and receptivity. According to the homogeneous principle, people seek a small group where they share some characteristics and feel they belong. This principle recognizes that the gospel travels with greater receptivity through friendship or kinship relationships. This has been documented by various studies that indicate that somewhere between 79 percent and 86 percent of all persons join a particular church because they were brought by a friend or family member. The age-graded Sunday School recognizes that people in the same stage of life share something in common. People in a similar age group generally have similar spiritual needs.

When I arrived in Norfolk, our adult Sunday School classes were not clearly graded on the basis of age. The people presently in Sunday School were not particularly interested in reorganizing the Sunday School along carefully graded lines. They had become comfortable with the groups that had been together for years. It was only when we found that visitors to Sunday School were having great difficulty finding a place to belong that we were willing to consider the need to age grade the school. We found that newcomers would visit two or three classes before we lost track of them. The various teachers assumed they had found a home in another class and thus were reluctant to follow up by contacting the visitors. Many visitors stopped attending. Some joined other churches while others were lost in the system. I am confident that many non-Christian visitors must have assumed that the church was not very interested in their spiritual needs.

When we finally summoned the courage to ask visitors why they had not joined our Sunday School, they responded that they were having difficulty finding a group to which they could belong. They were looking for a homogeneous group. For example, a new young couple that moves into a community is looking to develop friendships with other young couples of their age grouping. We can use the homogeneous principle to assist us with effective outreach.

The principle of homogeneity leads naturally to the companion *principle of receptivity.* The principle of receptivity suggests that the church should expend its greatest evangelistic energies on those who are most receptive to the gospel. We find the receptive principle illustrated when Jesus sent out His disciples with the instruction that they should shake the dust off their feet when they are not received at a home.

The age-graded Sunday School provides us with the opportunity of recognizing and creating natural receptivity. Persons who have visited your church, either through worship or Sunday School, have indicated both spiritual need and interest. They should be given immediate evangelistic attention. Our outreach program gave a high priority to responding to those who had visited our church and registered as guests.

We found that the Sunday School also enabled us to utilize receptivity to reach friends or family members of those attending. A woman who attended my wife's class was concerned about her husband's lost spiritual condition. She encouraged him to visit church or Sunday School with her. He did not object to her attending but would not come with her. Finally, with the help of her young daughter, she convinced him to attend a family picnic and swimming party sponsored by the Sunday School class. At the class party I met the young man and found out that we shared a common interest in old cars. Before the evening was over, he had invited my wife and me to their home for supper. He could hardly wait to show me his garage and the Corvette he was rebuilding. During the course of the evening I had the opportunity to lead him to accept Christ as personal Savior. Receptivity had been created through a Sunday School social.

An understanding of these twin growth principles led us to a strategy of assigning evangelistic visits through the Sunday School by age groups. I will discuss this strategy in greater detail below.

Advantage 2: Organizing through the Sunday School creates a multi-targeting approach to evangelism. Many church growth books give particular attention to targeting a particular age group, such as the Boomers or the Busters. Targeting simply means that you first understand the needs and interests of the age group you are attempting to reach, then you establish a strategy that will appeal to the needs and interests of that group. This will enable you to be more effective in sharing the gospel with them.

The age-graded Sunday School enables every church to utilize the principles of homogeneity and receptivity that are at the heart of targeting to reach a particular age group. The added bonus is that the age-graded

Sunday School allows you to target multiple age groups. In most cases this is essential since few churches can flourish by appealing to a single age group.

Advantage 3: Organizing through the Sunday School provides a simple, flexible, and workable plan for organizing outreach. The two keys to make the Sunday School outreach program effective are, (1) personal invitation by church members, and (2) assigning follow-up visits to the appropriate age-graded class. This plan makes the assignment of visits simple and natural and thus aids in accountability. Each visitor to church or Sunday School should be visited by a visitation team from his or her own age group. We discovered that this strategy made it simple to set up visitation appointments. Simplicity and flexibility make this evangelistic strategy easy to administer and to maintain.

Advantage 4: Organizing through the Sunday School takes advantage of the power of enrollment. My approach to Sunday School work was radically changed when I heard Andy Anderson, author of *The Growth Spiral,* talk about the advantages of open enrollment. He encouraged conference participants to enroll anyone in Sunday School who would give us permission. He then stated that attendance would grow in proportion to enrollment growth.

I took Andy at his word and began several enrollment campaigns at First Baptist, Norfolk. The results were essentially as he predicted: about half of those enrolled in Sunday School attended on a given Sunday. We enrolled many of our unsaved friends. We began to see a parallel growth curve in the number of baptisms on a yearly basis.

Curt Dodd made the same discovery when he was pastor of the fast-growing Metropolitan Baptist Church in Houston. He observed that two out of every three persons enrolled in Sunday School would be saved, whereas only one out of every 230 not enrolled in Sunday School would be saved.[8]

Yet when I presented this principle at various growth conferences, pastors called me afterwards, frustrated that they did not have the same growth results when they emphasized enrollment. In reading Chuck Kelley's book on the history of evangelism in the Southern Baptist Convention, I began to understand why the enrollment principle did not always yield growth results. Kelley noted that the "Action Plan," an enrollment program sponsored by the Sunday School Board, brought significant increases in enrollment but did not result in comparable gains in conversions and baptisms. The emphasis on enrollment during this program actually obscured the task of witnessing. People believed that simple enrollment could replace the need to share the gospel with the lost person. Kelley concluded that enrollment in a Sunday School focused on nurture may not yield the evangelistic results that it does in the Sunday School focused on evangelism.[9] The enrollment principle will work in evangelistically oriented Sunday Schools.

Advantage 5: Organizing through the Sunday School combats the tendency of the organization to stagnate. No matter what strategy you use for organizing your small-group Bible study, you will always fight the tendency of the organization to stagnate. Small groups soon become so introverted that newcomers find them hard to penetrate. The understanding that the goal of the Sunday School is evangelism will help you create new units and promote adults to the appropriate age group

What is your main purpose for Sunday School? Your answer will determine which actions you will reward. Is your main purpose to promote fellowship? If so, you won't establish new units because that might disrupt fellowship. If your main purpose for Sunday School is quality Bible teaching, you could make a good argument for placing all the adults in the auditorium and having the best-qualified teacher lecture on the Bible for an hour.

If your goal is a Great Commission Sunday School, then you will need to create new units that are based on the homogeneous principle. I am not suggesting that the evangelistic Sunday School cannot foster good fellowship and quality Bible study. I am merely emphasizing that the purpose of the Sunday School and the church is to faithfully fulfill the Great Commission. I suggest that the main purpose of Sunday School is to fulfill the Great Commission. I am arguing for a strategy that will allow you to address all three Great Commission concerns—evangelism, assimilation, and teaching.

Advantage 6: Organizing through the Sunday School gives you a sufficient reservoir of people to keep your outreach program functioning. The single greatest struggle related to visitation outreach is the maintenance of a sufficient number of volunteers to keep the program running efficiently. Most visitation programs begin with a high level of excitement and sufficient numbers of persons to follow up on all the visitors to the church and to visit other prospects. The initial excitement soon wanes and fewer and fewer persons participate in the visitation program. The same few loyal volunteers seem to bear the heavy weight of maintaining an effective visitation program.

Many churches have given up on visitation not because it doesn't work, but simply because they do not have enough people to maintain the program. The organization through the Sunday School does not guarantee an overabundance of volunteers, but it does help you in recruiting volunteers.

Organizing the Sunday School Visitation Program

I will deal primarily with the visitation program for adults, but the principles can be applied to the youth and older children's divisions of the Sunday School.

Our preschool outreach program was primarily aimed at reaching the unsaved parents of preschoolers and ministering to preschool families. Preschool visitation was often scheduled on Saturdays, once a month or more often if the need existed. Teachers and leaders should visit preschool families.

In our younger children's division we used a similar strategy. We also distributed quarterlies to the homes of all the children. This helped us to know the children in their home setting and to minister to parents.

Older children were normally visited through the adult outreach program since they were brought to church by a parent in most cases. If they came with a friend, we always sought the permission of their parent or guardian before making a visit to their home. If the children's leaders are not trained in evangelism, they should be accompanied by someone who has evangelism training.

Our youth often scheduled their outreach visitation on Wednesday nights after their fellowship time. Youth visited the youth who were prospects for their specific class. Youth usually were accompanied by their sponsors on visitation. We also trained youth in evangelism so that youth presented the gospel to other youth.

Our adult visitation was organized by the age-graded Sunday School classes. Our goal was to have a trained evangelism team from every Sunday School class at visitation each week. While we had a scheduled visitation night, we did allow teams to visit on other nights if it was more convenient for the team or the individual being visited.

If you utilize a training tool such as Evangelism Explosion or Continuing Witness Training, you should set a goal to have a trainer in every adult class. It is ideal if the trainers recruit their trainees from among fellow class members. We were not always able to achieve this goal, but it is the ideal. At this point we could draw our class organization chart as follows:

Training for Evangelism

The training strategy your church uses will be determined by the tool you choose to use to train laypersons to share their faith. A great majority of Christians will never effectively share their faith if they are not trained to do so. There are those who argue against the training programs that require participants to memorize an outline based on various Scripture passages. They claim that such approaches to sharing the gospel are "too canned." It is true that such an approach can sound memorized or canned. The difficulty is that most critics have not developed a better approach for training Christians to share their faith. The memorized approach should be seen as an outline on which Christians expand according to their own gifts and experience and according to the need of the moment. If we fail to give persons a system for sharing their faith, most will feel uncomfortable in doing so and probably avoid witnessing situations.

Most churches, particularly larger churches, will find that it is necessary to use a variety of training methods of varying lengths. Some programs demand a sixteen-week commitment. Work schedules will make this impossible for many of your church members. While we used Evangelism Explosion for our primary training tool, we also scheduled one-day training sessions on Saturdays that included an actual visitation opportunity. We also scheduled training sessions of varying durations during our regular Discipleship Training time.

The length of the study will often be determined by the training tool you use. You can teach someone to share a tract or mark a Bible for witnessing in a one-hour or two-hour session. We found that more people would attend the shorter, concentrated sessions and that some of these individuals would then enroll in the lengthier training programs.

The key is to find out what will work in your context. You can ask someone from a similar size church, or you can try various options until you find one that works for you. Most churches find that change helps keep the program fresh. For example, you may visit weekly during the school year, then change to a monthly emphasis during the summer when people's schedules are less predictable. You may also find that you will need to try several different visitation nights until you find the one that works best in your community. You will probably need to supplement the visitation program with other evangelistic strategies, such as evangelistic cell groups, power luncheons, fellowships for unsaved friends, and evangelistic events.[10]

Finding Prospects for Visitation

A second problem that some churches face is finding enough prospects to keep the evangelistic visitation program fueled. Nothing will destroy the outreach program more quickly than having people attend visitation but finding nobody assigned for them to visit. Evangelism training teams must have the opportunity to share the gospel in order to learn how to share the gospel.

Most growing churches and most larger churches will have enough visitors each week to keep their visitation teams fully scheduled. The church that has plateaued or is declining will have to work harder to discover prospects. Once the church begins to experience results from the visitation program and the church begins to grow, the number of visitors will also increase.

Finding prospects is not nearly so difficult as many would profess. People who need the gospel surround our churches. We have to find creative ways to build bridges that will enable us to share the gospel in a method appropriate to the need of the moment. Here are a few ideas that churches have found effective in finding prospects for visitation.

• Ask class members to list unchurched or unsaved friends on a 4 by 6 card. Encourage them to think about different environments in which these persons could be found, such as work, school, clubs, sports teams, and the like. This is most effective if it is done as part of a lesson on the needs of the unsaved.

• Schedule a Friend Day throughout the Sunday School. Ask everyone to bring one friend to Sunday School. The power of the personal invitation works, and many churches will find enough prospects to fuel visitation for several weeks out of this one event. The Friend Day must be well planned and promoted. The pastor and the teachers will be the key to success.

• Use special events appropriate to your community. Many churches have found that holidays provide great opportunities for scheduling big events. Living Christmas trees, Easter cantatas, and churchwide picnics are just a few of the big events to which people can bring friends. When I pastored in a rural setting, our church sponsored recreation events like softball and basketball games. We had parties for children as an alternative to Halloween. The event should be appropriate to your area, take advantage of the spiritual gifts of your church members, and be exciting enough that your members will want to bring their friends. The key to the success of the big event is the personal invitation by church members. It is also important to schedule follow-up visitation immediately after the big event. It is difficult to convince a prospect that you are vitally concerned about him or her if you take weeks to return their visit.

• Some churches have found community surveys to be productive. If the religious preference survey does not work well, consider a need-based survey. You can design your own by simply devising a few questions aimed at discovering needs your church might be prepared to meet. We discovered that people were more willing to talk to youth than to adults. We would occasionally combine a youth outing with survey work.

• Churches in larger communities have had good results with telephone surveys. The survey material is simply covered by a phone conversation rather than by a visit to the home. The church may choose to offer to mail appropriate information about the church if requested by the individual being called.

• Newcomers to your community are often looking for opportunities to make friends. A visit or call can often prove to be productive. Newcomer lists are available from numerous sources, including local realtors. We had good success with a more personal approach. We encouraged our members to watch for moving vans in their neighborhoods, and to respond with a personal visit. Some of our folk would take freshly baked cookies to their new neighbors.

• You should always capitalize on those who visit your church for any reason. Visitors to worship and Sunday School should be called and visited. Every church will need to determine the most effective way to register the visitors who attend church. The best way to register visitors is the one that works in your context. When you have special events, such as musical specials, you should always register visitors. You can accomplish this by asking everyone to fill out a special-events registration card. Prior to the event encourage your people to lead the way. Don't neglect opportunities like Vacation Bible School, children's choirs, youth camps, and other events where visitors may be present.

Implementing the Visitation Program

The first step in implementing the visitation program is to elect an outreach leader for each adult Sunday School class. Second, you should provide basic evangelism and visitation training for the outreach leaders. Third, the outreach leaders should recruit at least two persons to serve with them in organizing the class for outreach. Here is a possible job description for the outreach leader:

1. Pray for the unsaved by name.

2. Lead the class in identifying prospects.

3. Enlist and aid in the training of assistants for outreach.

4. Lead the class in outreach visitation.

5. Make weekly reports of contacts/visits.

6. Attend strategy planning and/or evangelism training—(strategy planning is discussed in chap. 9).

Someone in the church should be responsible for organizing the visitors' cards and making assignments of the visitors according to the appropriate age group. We collected visitors' cards during Sunday School and during worship. The cards were then copied on the appropriate map page from our city directory to assist the visitation team in locating the house.

Many visitors will be reluctant to give you their birthdate, but they are more than willing to circle the appropriate age group. Design your own visitor's card with a box to check according to the age grouping your

Sunday School is now using. Here is a sample of an age-specific card that will also help you determine the number and ages of the children in a specific family. Your card can be designed to indicate marital status if you have a singles ministry. The card will need to be changed as you grow and create new age groupings in Sunday School.

Name _____	
Home Phone _____	Work Phone _____
Address _____	
City _____	State ____ Zip _____
Recently moved from _____	
Church Membership _____	

Circle appropriate age group:

14-17	18-25	26-30	31-35	36-39	40-49	50-59	60+
Youth			Single			Married	

[ ] Please enroll me in Bible Study

Some recent growth conferences have convinced some pastors that it is difficult to get visitors to fill out visitors' cards. I never found this to be difficult, nor have a large number of pastors of growing churches. You should find a method that is comfortable for you to use in your community. Be natural and warm when you invite guests to register their attendance. There is no single right way to register guests. Some churches have the guests stand, others have them sit. Some have deacons stand and move through the congregation while visitors are encouraged to raise their hands. Some churches have had success by having all worship attenders, members and visitors alike, to sign a worship pad that is passed down the length of the row. You should experiment with several methods to find which works best for you.

Most effective evangelistic churches attempt to make several contacts with each prospect in a relatively short period of time. Here is a sample program, which resembles the one we used in Norfolk.

First contact: Doorstep visit of a deacon

A deacon makes an initial contact with visitors in his area of town on his way home from church. The deacon does not enter the house; he is only responsible for delivering a simple brochure that contains basic information about the church. If the family is at home, he personally delivers the brochure, thanks the visitor for attending, and indicates that someone will call to see when it would be appropriate to visit again. If no one is at home, the deacon leaves the brochure in the door with a handwritten personal note. We discovered that this initial visit prepared the visitor for the call to schedule the subsequent visit. If you do not have deacons or they have other ministry tasks, you should assign this visit to another group of persons.

Second contact: Staff member schedules personal visit

Sunday afternoon someone from the staff calls to see when it would be appropriate to schedule a personal follow-up visit. I found that the staff were much more effective in scheduling visits than were laity. Since First, Norfolk, was a large church, this also personalized the church. People frequently remarked, "I can't believe that someone from the staff called me." Before we had a large staff at Norfolk, I actually made all the calls myself. I found that I could make fifteen to twenty calls on a Sunday afternoon. It was not unusual for me to hear a visitor respond, "We visited four other churches before we came to First Baptist. You are the first church that has contacted us."

The content and the tenor of this call are vital. The caller should project a sense of excitement about the guest's attendance and about the church. You should assume that the guest is interested in the church. People today are unlikely to fill out a visitor's card if they are not open to some contact by the church. Here is a shortened sample conversation:

Hi, my name is _____. I am calling on behalf of (church name). We were delighted to have you visit with us today. I hope you enjoyed the service. It has been our practice to return the visit of those who have honored us with their presence. What would be an appropriate time for us to send someone from your age group by your home to tell you about the church and answer any questions you might have?

Notice three things:

• We offer the in-home visit in terms of hospitality.

• We do not ask a question that can be answered with a yes or no. Specifically, we do not ask, "May we send someone by to visit with you?" If you ask this question and they respond with a no, you are at the end of the conversation.

- We indicate that the visiting team will be someone from their age group. This activates the principle of homogeneity and creates receptivity.

You should take this as a basic outline and build on it according to your own personality and the specifics of each call. For example, if there were any details on the card that permitted dialogue, I would engage the visitor in a more lengthy dialogue to create receptivity. If I found that the visitor was from Nashville, and I had recently been to Nashville, I might mention that in the conversation. You will find your own style as you begin this activity. I think you will find this a most enjoyable ministry.

You may have noticed that I left the time of the church's return visit to our guest. Most respond by asking, "When do you regularly visit?" Thus most visits could be scheduled on the regular visitation night. If the regular visitation night posed a problem, we had persons who would visit at any time that was appropriate and convenient for the persons visiting the church. A large majority of our visits were actually scheduled before the visiting team left the church. This saved us a great deal of wasted energy and frustration. It also ensured the visitation team that the person(s) they were to visit were receptive.

I know that some of you may be thinking that personal visitation is the relic of a past generation. If you make a simple survey of the growing churches in your community or in America, you will discover that a large majority still have some form of visitation program. The problem is not that visitation no longer works. The problem is that most churches have no visitation program.[11]

Third contact: Sunday School class representative

The third contact is a call or personal note from a teacher or Sunday School outreach leader. In some instances a family might receive several phone contacts. If the visitors are a young couple with several children, the adult class teacher would call along with the teacher of the children. Instruct the teachers of children's classes to ask the parent's permission before they speak to the children directly. Parents today are very cautious about strangers speaking to their children.

Fourth contact: Visit of the visitation team

The next scheduled contact is that of the actual visitation team. The best team for this purpose will be persons from the Sunday School class that the visitor attended or would attend if he or she joined the church. Every team should have someone trained to share the gospel. We qualified everyone whom we visited to determine whether they had a personal relationship with Christ. Our first concern was not to encourage people to join our church, but to lead people to a saving knowledge of Christ. Some teams used Evangelism Explosion questions; other teams invited the persons being visited to share their personal testimonies. I have never known of born-again believers to be offended when someone asked them about their personal relationship with Christ. Besides, I would rather run the risk of offending someone than miss an opportunity to lead someone to Christ.

On outreach night each team picks up their visitation folder from their age-appropriate table. The folder contains a copy of the visitor's card, a map to the house, and all relevant information about the church. We color coded each folder according to the priority of the visit. A red dot designated a scheduled visit. A blue dot indicated a visitor from last week that we had been unable to contact by phone. A yellow dot indicated a visitor in recent weeks that we had not yet had the opportunity to visit. Yellow-dot folders could also include those who had been chronically absent from Sunday School or those who had visited the church through a recent large event. We encouraged all teams to take at least two folders that were in the same area of the city. This gave us a back-up visit in case the first family was not home.

Linking your evangelism program to the Sunday School class guarantees excellent follow-up. When our evangelism program was separate from the Sunday school, I struggled with the issue of follow-up visitation for those who made decisions for Christ. Most evangelism programs schedule only one follow-up visit. In many cases, that is simply not sufficient. Yet if you require the evangelism team to make several follow-up discipling visits, you will virtually cripple the evangelism training program. The linking of evangelism with the Sunday school help resolve this problem. When an evangelism team had the privilege to lead someone to Christ, we simply instructed them to spend the rest of the evening celebrating the occasion of the new birth. Instead of going through issues such as the importance of church membership and baptism, which often seemed anti-climatic to the excitement of the moment, we focused only on a single issue—the importance of Bible study for nurturing the new birth.

Here is a sample conversation:

We're excited to celebrate this moment with you! Is there anyone you would like to call and tell about this wonderful event? Why don't you call them right now? The Bible indicates that you are a new creature. Look at 2 Corinthians 5:17. You have been born again. Just like a newborn you will discover that you will have an insatiable appetite for spiritual things. First Peter 2:2 indicates that you will long for the Word of God like a newborn baby longs for milk.

The three of us belong to a small group of young adults your age that meet every Sunday morning at 9:30 to study the Bible. We would like you to join us in that small Bible study group. Can we count on you to join us next Sunday? We will take care of all the paperwork to enroll you in our class. We will be glad to meet you in the foyer at 9:15, take you to the class, and introduce you to other couples who are dealing with the same situations in life as you.

Notice that we actually enroll them in the Bible study class before they attend. Once they attend the Sunday School class they will be assigned to a care leader who will be responsible for the discipling of these new believers.

As you see, by linking our evangelism program with our Sunday School program, we resolved the dilemma of how to follow up on decisions for Christ during evangelistic visits. This was always a problem when our evangelism program was separate from the Sunday School organization.

A second dilemma occurs when the couple or individual being visited is not yet prepared to make a decision for Christ. Often evangelism teams, in their zeal to see decisions, persevere until they pluck fruit that isn't ripe for the harvest. In other cases, when the team leaves with no decision, it is difficult to know when to schedule a return visit. Often the people are forgotten as other visitors command attention. Because the visitation team originates in a Sunday School class, you can instruct the team to share the gospel as long as the visitor is receptive, they should not force the issue. If the visitation team senses that the fruit is not yet ripe for the harvest, they can end the visit by talking about the opportunity for the visitor to attend a small-group Bible study with other couples their own age.

This approach leaves the fruit unbruised and provides for a natural follow-up visit when appropriate. Once the couple or individuals attend Sunday School, they should be assigned to a care leader who regularly calls them to see how they are doing and what needs they might have.

You will often find that the unsaved couple will reschedule the evangelistic visit themselves. Remember, they are sitting in the same Sunday School class with the persons who came to visit them. We were able to enroll many of those who were not yet prepared to respond to the gospel.

Here is how this transition to a Sunday School conversation might sound:

> We are glad you invited us into your home and allowed us to share with you the most important discovery that we have ever made. We can understand your reluctance to make such a life-changing decision too quickly. We have all been right where you are tonight.

> The three of us belong to a small group of folk your age who are learning to cope with many of the same issues you are dealing with. We would love to have you join us in this Bible study group. It meets at 9:30 A.M. on the second floor of the church. I will be glad to meet you in the foyer this Sunday at 9:15 and take you to the class. We will all be there.

Fifth contact: Personal note from the visitation team

The visitation team should send a personal note thanking the people for the opportunity of visiting in their home and summarizing the results of the visit. If any persons prayed to receive Christ, reaffirm that decision and give them a Scripture verse to read. If you promised to meet them for Sunday School, remind them of the time and place.

Sixth contact: Visit of the Sunday School teacher

Once they have enrolled in Sunday School, they should be contacted by the teacher and given a quarterly or outline of study. This is best when it is done in person. The care leader and teacher should visit in the home when possible.

Seventh contact: Call from the care leader

The care leader should call the new Sunday School member on a regular basis to pray with him or her and to offer whatever assistance may be needed.

Conclusions

The Sunday School provides the most natural and effective way of organizing the church for ministry. If we look at its history, we will see that the Sunday School was most effective when its primary purpose was outreach.

Sunday School is not a relic or a fossil; it is simply not being used for the purpose for which it was created.

The Sunday School is a simple, flexible, and workable outreach tool that maximizes the principles of homogeneity and receptivity, employs a multitargeting approach, takes advantage of the power of enrollment, combats stagnancy, and provides a sufficient reservoir of volunteers to keep the program functioning.

To make the Sunday School function as an outreach tool requires an organizational strategy for the entire school. Every adult class should have an elected outreach leader who understands and accepts his or her responsibilities.

The church will need to develop a practical and suitable plan for training laity to share their faith effectively. Most churches will employ a wide variety of methods to discover prospects. This is a much easier task than many people realize.

The church must make these commitments, then implement the strategy. The Sunday School strategy offers many advantages that overcome the problems often connected with aggressive outreach programs.

By using the Sunday School as an outreach tool, you will soon begin to experience growth. Since much of this growth will be conversion growth, we must now consider how to assimilate new people through the Sunday School.

&

SEVEN

The Ministry of Assimilation

The closest thing to Heaven, while living life this side of the grave, should be the fellowship of Christians living in community. Believers should be bearing burdens, sharing joys, and richly enjoying the good things of God with the hope that someday, maybe soon, joy will no longer be mixed with pain and suffering. But for now, a grief shared is half a grief; a joy shared is a greater joy."[1]

This quotation from the book *The Church in Ruins*, by William Crabb and Jeff Jernigan, strikes a note of empathy. We all long to share in a true Christian community, but we have found authentic community to be in short supply. Crabb and Jernigan themselves note that the church rarely offers the sort of biblical community it advertises and alone has the potential to provide. Lyle Schaller found that at least one third, and perhaps as many as one half, of all Protestant church members do not feel a sense of belonging to the congregation of which they are members. They have been received as members, but they have never felt that they have been accepted into the fellowship circle of the church.[2]

Crabb and Jernigan point to the biblical model from the Book of Acts and argue that there are four basics for Christian community. The first is teaching, with the apostles' doctrine at its core. They correctly note that right living flows from right belief. The second issue is Christian fellowship, which is equally vital. They argue that community may be God's key means of sustaining the values that keep faith pure and our species surviving. The third and fourth biblical elements of Christian community are worship and prayer.[3]

I believe that a Bible study organization combined with an exciting worship service provides the church of today, and will provide the church of tomorrow, with the finest organizational strategy to build Christian community; thus, it will effectively assimilate new members as well as provide ongoing ministry to all members.

This chapter begins with the issue of assimilation because assimilation is essential to conserving the results of evangelism. Without assimilation, the opportunity for ongoing discipleship training will not exist. My conviction is that assimilation is an ongoing concern of the church and will ultimately cause the church to address the issue of discipleship. For that reason, I will also suggest a discipling strategy that can be customized to fit the needs of your church.

The Case for an Assimilation Strategy

1. You do not have a choice. Lyle Schaller has perceptively observed that the key question is not whether we are going to develop an assimilation plan. Every church has a plan; some plans are simply worse than others.

Once the church grows beyond about thirty-eight persons, assimilation becomes a critical issue since that is the sphere of knowledge of any one person.[4] The church that is smaller than thirty-eight members functions like a single-cell entity, and people are easily assimilated. As the church grows beyond this figure, people will not be assimilated automatically. The ultimate question then is whether you have a plan that works efficiently.

2. Assimilation is a biblical mandate. We could first point to the threefold strategy necessary for obedience to the Great Commission. We are called to make disciples by going, baptizing, and teaching. If going points to the task of evangelism, then baptizing focuses on assimilation. Baptism is not just an ordinance required for membership in some churches, it is an act of obedience that symbolizes the incorporation of the new believer into the body of Christ, the church.

In an attempt to counter the divisive bickering of the Corinthians, Paul pointed to their common baptismal experience. Listen to that verse in context: "For even as the body is one and yet has many members, and all the members of the body, though they are many, are one body, so also is

Christ. For by one Spirit we were all baptized into one body, whether Jews or Greeks, whether slaves or free, and we were all made to drink of one Spirit. For the body is not one member, but many" (1 Cor. 12:12–14).

I frequently speak of baptizing as *congregationalizing*. What strategy do you have to baptize or congregationalize those you are privileged to reach?

3. Assimilation is necessary if evangelism is to survive and thrive. Every church with a heart for evangelism must be concerned about assimilation. We are all incensed when we read about parents who abandon a newborn. Perhaps they left the child on someone else's doorstep, or they may have callously crammed the child into a desolate dumpster. In either case we are appalled by such insensitivity. We may find ourselves saying, "People shouldn't have children they aren't willing to nurture. Those folk should have thought about their responsibility for the child before they conceived a baby." That is precisely my argument about assimilation. If a church has no intention or plan to care for the newborn Christian, it will not sustain the excitement for evangelism.

Perceptive members of the church will readily see that evangelistic results do not translate into church growth. I have seen churches that boasted about large numbers of conversions year after year, yet those churches show little evidence of growth in Bible study, mission giving, or other significant components of healthy growth. This can lead to disillusionment and apathy. In such a church, any outreach program will be difficult to sustain.

A lack of attention to assimilation can also lead to a lack of confidence in the power of the gospel. If church members see people making public professions of faith, but they do not see them incorporated into the church with an accompanying lifestyle change, they may begin to question whether people are really being saved and why the gospel does not appear to exert much power in the lives of these people.

4. Assimilation is a necessary prerequisite for discipleship. Simply stated, you cannot teach people to observe all that Christ commanded if they are not present. People must first feel that they belong before they can be brought to a mature expression of their faith. The teaching ministry of the church will be severely hampered if there is not an effective strategy for assimilation.

5. Assimilation is a key element of church growth. Kirk Hadaway's extensive research revealed that growing churches are more likely to have an assimilation strategy through which they keep up with their members.

"They are more likely to have a deacon family ministry plan or a zone plan, for instance . . . . 75 percent of growing churches have such a plan in operation as compared to 58 percent of plateaued churches and 43 percent of declining congregations."[5] Assimilation aids church growth by conserving the results of evangelism and providing the opportunity for discipleship.

The Keys to Effective Assimilation

Before we address the matter of design, we should first pay attention to key assimilation issues. What do we mean by assimilation? What is required for an effective assimilation strategy?

We are fortunate that there have been numerous studies of assimilation. Kirk Hadaway argues that there are four key components to assimilation: (1) keep people involved in small groups and build relationships, (2) meet their needs, (3) avoid making them mad and/or help them resolve their anger, and (4) overcome the perception that no one cares.[6]

Gary McIntosh and Glen Martin, in their book *Finding Them, Keeping Them,* noted that many of the churches that are inclusive in their outreach were nonetheless exclusive in their fellowship. They therefore suggest that an effective assimilation strategy be built on five blocks: building friendships, involving members in tasks/roles, participation in small groups, helping newcomers identify with the purpose of the church, and fostering spiritual growth among individuals.[7]

Lyle Shaller found that every congregation can be described by the use of two concentric circles. "The larger outer circle is the membership circle. Every member is within that circle. The small inner circle includes the members who feel a sense of belonging and who feel fully accepted into the fellowship of that called-out community. Most of the leaders come from persons within this fellowship circle. By contrast, many of the workers who do not have policy-making authority may be drawn from among the members who are outside the fellowship circle."[8] Assimilation then means the strategy of drawing all our members into that inner circle. It is the process of lifelong attachment of believers to the local body of Christ.

Assimilation is not all that complex. *People need to feel that they are wanted, that they belong, and that they are needed.* For this to occur they will need to be incorporated in the church through a small group where these dynamics can occur. In turn, for this to happen systematically, there must be a plan of action. It is true that some outgoing people will assimilate themselves by sheer dent of personality, but for every self-assimilator we find there will be several persons who will drop by the wayside if they are not offered assistance in the assimilation process.

This chapter suggests an assimilation plan based on the Sunday School. It can be tailored to meet the needs of any church of any size. Use it only as a guideline, and mold it to fit your own unique context.

Utilize the Sunday School

The assimilation task cannot be accomplished without the use of small groups. You may attract people through the "front door" of exciting worship, but you will not assimilate them through worship alone. If people are to feel wanted and needed, they must find identity with your church through involvement in a small group.

Most churches will have multiple small groups already functioning. The choir, for example, provides a small-group experience for many persons. Committees, support groups, prayer groups, governing boards, and the like can all fulfill a small-group function for many people in your church. Nonetheless, not everyone will automatically find their way into such a support group. You must have an overarching strategy that ensures that everyone can be assimilated through a small-group relationship. Many persons will actually participate in several small groups. This redundancy helps to provide a fail-safe system to ensure that no one falls through the cracks. The small-group Bible study organization provides the most comprehensive system for ensuring that everyone has a small group experience.

Kirk Hadaway, in his research on assimilation, discovered that churches with effective programs of assimilation utilized the standard age-graded Sunday School.

> For older churches the task is to make sure that open groups exist and that new members are channeled to these groups. This is essential to church growth. Baptist churches often do this by a rigidly enforced age grading of Sunday School and through the addition of new classes. By limiting the duration that a member spends in a group and by regular promotion of members from department to department or class to class, the church is able to keep (or at least retard) social groups from becoming too rigid and unable to accept newcomers. Since classes receive promotees on an annual basis, accepting new members from outside the church may be easier than in churches which do not make the effort to promote adult Sunday School members. Churches which use

standard age-grading procedures and which divide classes tend to grow. Research clearly supports such a conclusion.[9]

The reasons that the age-graded Sunday School has proven to be such an effective tool for the assimilation of new members are relatively simple and straightforward. First, age grading creates both homogeneity and receptivity. Second, age-grading keeps the small groups from becoming stagnant and thus calcifying. Virtually every study on small-group dynamics indicates that the longer a particular group stays together, the harder it is for a newcomer to penetrate that group. Most small groups reach a saturation point within twelve to eighteen months. The age grading and regular promotion of all Sunday School classes will counteract the tendency toward fossilization.

Before you look to build another organization for the assimilation of new members, may I recommend that you look first to your Sunday School.

Use the Power of Personal Invitation

You cannot replace the power of the personal invitation and intentional enrollment as the twin keys to success in the assimilation process. These two principles go hand in hand to ensure that assimilation is both personal and comprehensive.

If we accept the generally agreed-upon finding that somewhere between 79 percent and 86 percent of the people who join a local church do so because of the invitation of a friend or family member, then we should utilize the power of the personal invitation to aid in the task of assimilation. It is for this very reason that I suggest that the outreach and inreach or assimilation program be tied to the age-graded Sunday School. If someone invites a new member to join their small-group Bible study group, the chances of involvement are greatly increased. You should encourage those in outreach to issue personal invitations to join a Sunday School class, and you should assign someone to call or visit everyone who has joined the church and invite them to attend the appropriate class.

This invitation must be personal, genuine, and immediate. If someone joins your church during a worship service this Sunday, someone should be assigned to call and invite the person to your small-group Bible Study before its next scheduled meeting. Here again, receptivity will be greatly enhanced if you utilize the principle of homogeneity. Someone from the class that the newcomer would attend should extend the personal invitation. The person calling should offer to meet the first-time attender at a particular place and accompany them to the appropriate class. The newcomer is often unsure of where to find his or her class and may be intimidated about the prospect of walking into a room full of strangers.

Universal enrollment will help stop leaks

Every church struggles with the leaks that allow people to drop out of involvement without being noticed. This problem increases as the church grows in numerical size. I can still remember staff meetings when someone would ask about a particular family. As we discussed their needs, we would realize that no one had seen them recently. *When the task is assumed to be the responsibility of everyone, it becomes the concern of no one.* By the time we made the contact, the situation that had led to their inactivity had often escalated to the point of no return. We knew that we had to have a more systematic and comprehensive way to assure that everyone was cared for. This led to our strategy for universal enrollment, a plan for enrolling every church member in a small group for assimilation, Bible study, and discipleship.

It is a simple matter to enroll newcomers. First, they join with an enthusiasm to be involved. Second, once universal enrollment is established, you can simply assign new member to a small group.

The greatest hurdle in implementing universal enrollment is the decision about what you should do with those present members who are not enrolled in a small group. Each church might handle the enrolling of present members in a slightly different fashion.

A word of caution. You might be tempted to think that members who are actively participating in the church but not in a small group for Bible study have formed their own assimilation network. Thus you could choose the philosophy, "If it ain't broke, don't fix it." However, as a church increases in size, this strategy will become less successful.

In the small church, chronic absence of an active member can be detected by sight in the worship center. Someone will notice that a particular couple isn't sitting in their regular seats. Thus someone, often the pastor, will call to see if there is a need. As size increases, this visual-care ministry becomes increasingly difficult. You will begin to find that a comprehensive strategy for assimilation and care must be implemented for everyone.

I would recommend that you simply enroll everyone in a small group based on their age group. If you have good church records, birth dates should be readily available.

You may be thinking that you have some people who would leave the church if assigned to a group without their consent. While I cannot guarantee that this will never occur, I can assure you that the positive effects far outweigh the possible negative ramifications. People who would be offended by a church's desire to implement a strategy for caring for newcomers and church members will ultimately be offended by something else. You cannot make every decision based on its potential for offending someone or you'll never do anything.

You can implement the strategy with minimal conflict if you clearly communicate the need and the plan. Connect the strategy with the mandate of the Great Commission. Discuss the need with various groups of leaders and develop a consensus. You can explain that while attendance at small-group Bible study can neither be forced nor enforced, the need for universal enrollment is based on the church's desire to care for its total membership. This will dull any attack that you are simply trying to inflate enrollment numbers. For this to have credibility you must follow through on the plan for ministry. You will have accomplished nothing but disappointment if you enroll everyone in a small group and then fail to implement the caring ministry.

Hints for enrolling present members

Let me list a few ideas for enrolling members who are not now involved in a small group.

1. *Ask your deacons, elders, church council, or other ruling bodies to vote to endorse the plan.* Churches that have regular business conferences should bring the idea for a church vote. Even if your church doesn't require such a vote, the consensus of the congregation needs to be built for the plan to work properly.

2. *Notify all the members about the plan, explaining how assignments will be made.* Detail the advantages of the program, even for persons who choose not to attend the small group to which they have been assigned. It will probably require several notifications before people fully understand the plan. Use the church newsletter, bulletin inserts, handouts, and personal letters to communicate with the people.

3. *Have the care teams from the classes visit all the members assigned to their particular care group.* Ask them to explain the value of the program and invite nonattenders to join them for Bible study. We found an interesting reaction about our enrollment campaign from some of our less active

members. They commented that this was the only aggressive visitation/contact campaign the church had ever conducted that didn't ask them for money. After a few moments to ponder the response, I realized they were correct. Its true, we're not reluctant to send letters and make visits to ask people to pledge to the budget or building fund, but we are reluctant to visit them to invite them to attend Bible study. I recommend the personal visit strategy. You will find that you will positively touch more people than you will offend.

4. Customize any strategy to fit your local situation. You may be in an area where a mail campaign plus a calling campaign is more feasible and constructive. You will have to be the judge of strategy.

Hints for enrolling new members

1. Many new members will be enrolled and assimilated in Sunday School before they actually join the church. This is particularly the case where open enrollment (the process of allowing anyone to enroll in a small group) is practiced and visitation is closely tied to the Sunday School. Over time we found that many of the people who joined our church had been members of the Sunday School for some time.

2. Enroll others during the new-member counseling. Churches have different practices concerning the receiving of new members. Some will receive them immediately into the fellowship, while others will offer some new-member counseling or training prior to formally receiving persons for membership. In either case, every church should have both new-member counseling and new-member training. New-member counseling simply ensures that individuals making a particular commitment understand fully the decision they are making. New-member training is more involved and should include information about the church, its mission and beliefs, and material on spiritual growth.

In churches with a tradition of public invitation, the first opportunity for counseling is at the moment an individual responds to the invitation to accept Christ or join the church. We found that it was best to take everyone to a private counseling area so that we could deal with their unique needs. As part of our conversation with new members, we asked them if they were currently enrolled in a small group for Bible study in our church. If they answered yes, we simply noted the group and the teacher. If they answered no, we explained the importance of small-group Bible study for assimilation and spiritual growth and assigned them to the appropriate class. In our case, assignment was made based on the age of the wife. Here again, the age-graded organizational strategy greatly simplifies the work of assimilation.

To my knowledge we never had a new member reject the offer to enroll in a Bible study. This does not mean that all of them attended every Sunday, but it does mean they knew they were assigned to a group for Bible study and personal care. (See p. 167 for the form we used to make and record assignments.)

3. Inform the teacher and the appropriate care leader of the persons who have been assigned to their class.

4. Make an assimilation visit within the week. The assimilation visit differs from the outreach visit in its purpose. The outreach visit is aimed at evangelism or church membership. In the case of the assimilation visit, the individual is already a member of the church. The purpose of this visit is to facilitate the entry of the new member into the small-group structure of the church. This visit is casual and may include the delivery of Bible study materials, information on the location of the class, and notification of any class events such as class socials or prayer groups.

The visiting team should offer to meet the new members at a central location and accompany them to their classes on their first Sunday. The visitation team should give testimony of the importance of the small group in their own spiritual growth and have prayer with the new members.

5. Once the new member is enrolled there should be regular contact and ministry through the care groups (see below).

Integrating assimilation and new-member training

Every church should have some program for new-member training and orientation. In the smaller church this may be as brief as several hours of orientation. The larger and more complex the church becomes, the greater the amount of time required. Most churches will need to design their own material and to decide when this can best be accomplished.

In the most basic program, the new member should be acquainted with the history of the church as well as the vision for the future. This is an excellent opportunity to help people buy into the purpose of the church. An orientation to the building is usually of great value. We tend to take for granted that people can find their own way around and understand our jargon. How does a newcomer know that the "sanctuary" is a place for people to worship and not an asylum for birds?

An explanation of the program and meeting times is essential. Here again, you will probably need to translate your jargon for new members. Don't presume that new members understand the names of your church programs or denominational emphases.

New-member orientation and training is an excellent time to review the important doctrines, ordinances and/or sacraments of your church or denomination. Even if this is review material for many of your new members, it does not hurt to teach by repetition.

New believers, as opposed to those joining from another church or denomination, should also be exposed to some of the basic discipling material that would help them understand the new birth and how to grow in their faith. This probably should be separated from new-member orientation. This can be accomplished through small groups that are different from the Sunday School structure, or it can be facilitated through the care group structure.

The scheduling of the new-member orientation classes will need to be customized to each local church. In the early days of our growth at First Baptist, Norfolk, we held these classes during the Sunday School hour. This was a convenient time and helped to develop the habit of attending both Sunday School and worship. Our orientation classes were six weeks in duration. The greatest drawback was that it took new members out of their age-graded classes, the natural place of assimilation. We found that this was particularly objectionable to our single members. We later moved to a Sunday and Wednesday night schedule. In our mobile society, you will probably find that it will be necessary to offer several different options to meet the scheduling needs of many of your members.

Care Ministry Teams

Every class should be organized for the personal care of all its members. The level of care will be determined by the need of the individual. The care ministry can be organized through the Sunday School, but it will require commitment, training, supervision, and accountability. It will also require ministry outside the classroom.

What is a care group?

A care group is simply a grouping of people for the expressed purpose of making regular contacts for prayer, communication, and the discovery and meeting of needs. The most natural place for care groups to function is through your Bible study organization.

What is the optimum size for a care group?

The optimum size for a care group is three to four persons or couples. We tried to assign a larger number of couples, but found that the system experienced too many failures. If the care leader is responsible for making weekly contacts, a large number will create a sense of paralysis. The care leaders will get behind and choose to contact no one rather than to contact only a portion of their families. Administrative studies have shown that a good supervisor can handle three to four persons in a supervisory capacity. The same principle holds for care leaders.

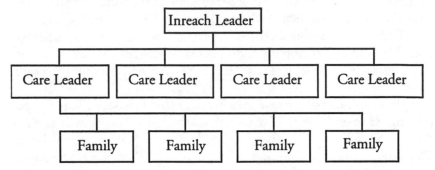

This means that a men's Sunday School class that has twenty-four persons enrolled would need to have six care leaders. If this were a couples class, you would only need three care leaders. In a couples class the care leader would be responsible for four couples. One call actually makes two contacts in the couples class. Some churches have chosen to have a few larger classes along with the traditional-sized class (twenty to twenty-five enrolled). The key to the success of the larger class is the expansion of the care group structure to provide ample care leaders to meet individualized needs. You should still retain the same one-to-four ratio.

In every class you need an inreach leader for every four care leaders. This individual provides oversight for and cares for the care givers. At First, Norfolk, we attempted to do this task with the deacons. This required that deacons become ministry oriented rather than administration oriented. We believed that this ministry task fit the description for deacon ministry in Acts 6. You do not have to use deacons to accomplish this work, but you do need to have someone in place to care for the care givers and to hold them accountable or the system will break down.

For the care system to work, it should mirror the organizational structure of the Sunday School. In other words, there is a need for a departmental deacon or care captain. These individuals care for the class deacons or care leader captains. In the larger church where there might be several departments in the young adult division, there might also be a divisional care captain. Let me illustrate both the class structure and a department structure. You can then customize a system that will fit your needs.

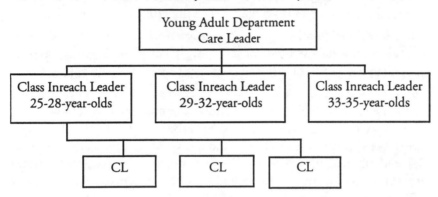

What is the task of the care leader?

The care leader's primary responsibility is to care for the needs of those assigned to his or her group. The level of care should be based on the needs of the individual. This care make take several forms.

1. The care leader should call or contact all members each week. Many care leaders make the mistake of contacting only absentees. This does not affirm those who attend weekly, it can lead to discouragement for the care leader, and it may cause you to miss ministry opportunities. Calls and personal notes can be used to maintain contact with members. The personal call should be the primary tool since it allows for interaction and personal prayer. Care leaders should be encouraged to pray for needs over the phone. The care-leader call is not primarily a call to encourage attendance, it is a call to provide ministry. Regular attendance will often be the outcome of caring ministry, but it should not be the goal.

2. The care leader should be sure that a personal visit is made when a new person is assigned to a care group. Assignments are made by the inreach leader in each class. The purpose of the initial personal visit is to get to know the new member of the care group and to encourage each one to be a vital participant in the small group. Additional visits should be made according to need or request. For example, the care leader should visit if there is a special need, such as a birth, death, or serious illness. When a personal visit is made, the care leader should always visit with a companion. It is ideal if the husband and wife visit together. The care leader and inreach leader or teacher may form the visitation team. If these role assignments put a man and woman who are not married to each other together, there must be a third member of the visitation team.

3. *There are times when a personal note or special card may be sufficient to meet the need.* A handwritten note can simply state that the group has been missing them. A card on a birthday or anniversary is always appreciated.

4. *Each care leader should keep careful records of all visits, calls, and contacts.* The records should include matters like ministry needs, prayer concerns, and caring activities. The care leader should know about and remember special occasions like birthdays, wedding and death anniversaries, and other significant days. These are important contact and ministry opportunities. The care leader should keep this information in a ministry folder or notebook.

5. *On some occasions the care leader may need to share with the class a prayer or ministry need.* The care leader should work with the inreach leader or deacon to organize the class for ministry action. For example, the class should provide meals at the time of a death. The care leader can share the need, collect the food, and make the distribution.

6. *Care leaders should be trained not to share prayer concerns given in confidence without permission.* The care leader is not expected or trained to be a pastoral counselor. Thus when a care leader finds a need that requires personal or family counseling, he or she should ask for permission to share this need with their inreach leader, deacon, or pastor. This will enable the pastor to know about ministry needs and to meet those needs before they become critical.

7. *The care leader should report to the class inreach leader the results of ministry contacts.* This assures that accountability will be maintained. The inreach leader will be able to detect when any care group is not functioning. Here again, confidentiality must be guarded.

8. *The fundamental tasks of the discipling ministry will be accomplished through an effective caring ministry.* I think that many churches are ineffective in the discipling task because they fail to understand and apply the discipling hierarchy of needs (see the following table). The formative level of discipling needs—bonding, nurturing, and spiritual self-worth—are best

accomplished by a one-on-one strategy.[10] Every new Christian should be assigned to a care leader. These individuals will need closer monitoring during the early stages of the Christian experience. The care leader should offer to sit with them in worship, encourage them in their personal Bible study, and offer to pray with them and for them. While this creates a heavier load of responsibility, in most churches each care leader would only have one or two persons a year who are new believers. Besides, this is the most exciting and rewarding aspect of the caring ministry.

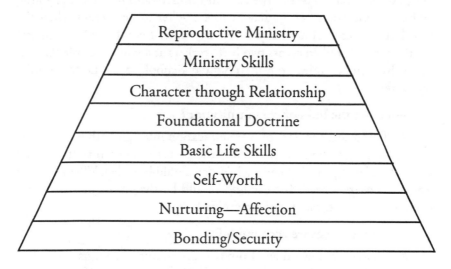

Reproductive Ministry

Ministry Skills

Character through Relationship

Foundational Doctrine

Basic Life Skills

Self-Worth

Nurturing—Affection

Bonding/Security

As a pastor, I cannot endorse this caring strategy too strongly. First, Norfolk, grew quickly from 380 average Sunday School attendance to over 2,000 in a nine-year period. It would have been an overwhelming pastoral care task if we had not discovered this caring strategy through the Sunday School. When a ministry need occurred, it was the norm for the Sunday School class members to be the first to respond. I would be called to a hospital room only to find that the care leader, class deacon, or teacher was already present. The class often notified me of the ministry needs. This prevented me from the embarrassment that every pastor fears—not hearing about a death or hospitalization before it is too late to offer ministry.

The stories of care leader ministry are numerous. Once, my wife Paula and I arrived home from our national convention only to discover that one of the young ladies in her class was in the hospital ready to give birth to twins prematurely. The class members had already responded in our absence. They had notified the prayer chain, inquired about possible ministry needs among other family members, and sent flowers and cards. The call for ministry that came to our home was not for me as pastor but for my wife as the Sunday School teacher. It was a joy to watch her minister to that young woman in a way that I would never have been capable of ministering. Both babies eventually died. The night the last living child was about to die, the nurse from the neonatal intensive care called our home requesting to speak to Paula. The nurse, who was not a member of our church, had seen the class in ministry and felt that the young woman would want her Sunday School teacher to be present when she heard of the death of her baby. A few days later I conducted the funeral for the twins. I looked across two little caskets at a young couple flanked by twelve other couples from their Sunday School class. The care ministry works!

What are the lines of communication?

We found that the lines of communication must go both ways for the caring ministry to be effective. When the pastor or church staff member hears of a ministry need, the inreach leader should be called. When the care leader discovers a need that can and should be shared, he or she should make sure the pastor and staff are notified.

How do you ensure accountability?

Accountability flows down from the top. In our case we used the deacon ministry group along with the Sunday School structure for organization and accountability. If your church has a different task for deacons or does not have deacons, you can develop the same system but use different persons and titles.

The pastor can call the chairman of deacons and simply ask about spiritual needs in the congregation he should be aware of or praying for. He might also enquire about the activity of the care ministry. The chairman of the deacons would in turn call the department or division deacons or care captains and ask for a report. The process would continue down the line to the level of the care leader. Here again, the communication process must move in both directions.

If some of the caregivers along the chain of responsibility regularly fail to accomplish their task, they are probably serving in an area for which they are not gifted. For the sake of the health of the body, they should be replaced. The need for replacing caregivers will be greatly diminished if they are recruited and trained with a full understanding of their responsibilities.

How do you assign persons to a care group?

In our case assignments were made through the age-graded Sunday School system. The deacon in that class would assign the class members to a care leader. An attempt was made to make assignments with a view to fairness. Some persons assigned in care groups will be inactive members. Some of those may be angry or disillusioned. If too many inactive persons are assigned to one group, the care leader could easily become discouraged.

What does the care leader do if someone asks not to be bothered?

Obviously you cannot force ministry on anyone. The care leader may choose to only contact such persons once a quarter to see how they are doing. The leader might send birthday cards to them. The care leader can assure the individuals that he or she will continue to pray for them. In some cases all you can do is wait until a ministry need arises and then re-establish contact.

How do you train care leaders?

The training will vary according to the individual setting. I would suggest that you take the eight tasks listed above, print out a job description, and develop your own training program and materials. If you select persons who have a clear understanding of the role of care leaders and who possess the gifts for caring ministry and the desire to do the tasks, a great deal of training will not be required.

Meet with the care leaders, go over the job description, and give suggestions for how to make a caring call. Show them examples of notes that express concern. The inreach leaders and care leaders should meet regularly, and pray together and encourage one another. Much of the training will continue as they grow through ministry experience.

What is the role of the inreach leader or deacon?

The work of the leader of the care ministry in the class is essentially the same as the care leader, with additional administrative responsibilities. The care captain or inreach leader enlists the care leaders, helps with the training of care leaders, assigns class members to care groups, ensures that caring ministry is occurring, reports to the department care captain, assists care leaders to mobilize the class for special care projects, and provides the care ministry for the class care leaders.

Conclusion

Assimilation is the fulcrum on which the ministries of evangelism and discipleship are balanced. Without an adequate plan for assimilation, neither evangelism nor discipleship will be effective in the long term. The local church must choose to be proactive about assimilation because it is demanded by the Word of God.

The age-graded Sunday School organization provides an excellent skeletal structure on which to construct an effective assimilation program. You must begin by enrolling all church members in a small group for nurture. Once enrolled, every member should be assigned to a care leader who will keep in regular contact, assess ministry needs, and help facilitate the appropriate ministry actions.

さ

EIGHT

The Ministry of Teaching

The Sunday School experience must be an enjoyable and profitable one if participants are going to attend with regularity and be enthusiastic about bringing their friends. For these goals to be reached each class must maintain a balance of teaching, caring, outreach, and fellowship. The teacher is the point person in ensuring that this balance is maintained. Thus Sunday School teachers should not be selected solely on the basis of their Bible knowledge and communication ability. While these are important, they reflect only a part of the overall task of the Sunday School and the teacher. This is not to suggest that the teacher is to accomplish all the work of the Sunday School, but it is to say that he or she must support and facilitate all the work. The parallel example would be that of the pastor of the church. He cannot do all the tasks of ministry, but he is responsible for coordinating and facilitating them.

It is important that the teacher understand that his or her role involves more than the delivery of a forty-minute Bible study each week. The teacher is the leader of the class, and as such, he or she must become the catalyst that makes the Great Commission strategy function and the class operate as a single unit. The teacher is the key to the functioning of the class and therefore must fully understand and embrace the concept of the Great Commission Sunday School.

You should select and train teachers who are team players. A clear understanding of the role of the teacher should be at the forefront of the recruitment and training process. The teacher should be positively passionate about the function of the Sunday School and the mission and vision of the church. A teacher has a great opportunity to aid the church in reaching its goals and accomplishing its mission. On the other hand, a teacher who is out of step with the congregational goals and teaching can cause great damage.

Let's look together at several facets of the teaching ministry of the Sunday School. Since this chapter by its very nature can be only an overview, I would recommend two other books for those involved in the teaching ministry: Daryl Eldridge, ed., *The Teaching Ministry of the Church* (Nashville: Broadman & Holman, 1995), and Findley Edge, *Teaching for Results* (Nashville: Broadman & Holman, 1995.

Establishing Goals as a Teacher

Clear goals and guidelines will aid the teacher in accomplishing the tasks necessary for the Sunday School class to successfully fulfill its purpose. Clear goals will also enable the church to be more effective at recruiting teachers. I would suggest that you utilize the seven goals that follow as a beginning guideline for developing a job description for your teachers. You may need to add other specific goals as they relate to your church or denomination.

The teacher will teach the Bible effectively

The first goal of the teacher must be to teach the Bible with conviction and excitement. To do so the teacher must first be a good student of the Bible. Learners always make the best teachers. This would suggest that the teacher should be committed to lifelong learning, which would involve regular participation in training sessions and regular meetings. Even though the Great Commission Sunday School has several functions, the teaching of the precious Word of God is at its heart. It is the Bible that is quick and powerful, like a two-edged sword. It is the Bible that brings conviction of sin. The gospel is the power of God unto salvation. The Bible is the record of God's revelation of Himself to man. It is not so much the persuasiveness of the teacher that makes a Sunday School lesson powerful, it is the power of the Word of God taught plainly and with conviction under the inspiration of the Holy Spirit.

Marion Brown and Marjorie Prentice conducted a study of one hundred Southern Baptists. First they asked them why they come to Sunday School. Of those questioned, 98.9 percent answered that they attend to learn more about the Bible. When asked why they attend a particular class, 93.5 percent said because the teacher knows the Bible.[1]

The teacher must first make a commitment to teach the Bible under the power of the Holy Spirit.[2] Don't forget that our teaching goal is to bring about lifestyle change that is motivated by an understanding of God's Word.

The teacher will embody the lesson

Nothing is more powerful than an object lesson that accompanies the taught lesson. The object lesson must be the transformed life of the teacher. This should not be construed to mean that the teacher must be perfect to qualify to teach. We are all on a spiritual pilgrimage to be conformed to the image of Christ. There are, nonetheless, certain essentials that must be non-negotiables.

The teacher must have a clear testimony of a personal relationship with Jesus Christ and be one who actively shares that faith. It will be virtually impossible to develop a strong evangelistic climate in the Sunday School class if the teacher doesn't embody the biblical principles related to witnessing.

The teacher should model the Christian home. Here again it will be impossible to teach with conviction about the importance of the family and the home if the teacher does not care for these basic relationships. The stable Christian home is one of the arenas where the church must have an effective witness.

The teacher should practice the Christian disciplines and should give evidence of spending personal time alone with God. The teacher should be known as a person of prayer and devotion. This will give life, conviction, and personality to the teaching. He or she will not be teaching from a lifeless book of history, but from a book that has come alive through personal experience.

The teacher should be a committed churchgoer. Corporate worship, biblical stewardship, and loyalty to the mission of the church will enable the teacher to teach with personal conviction. At one point in a period of rapid growth at Norfolk, we incorporated several lessons on biblical stewardship into our ongoing Sunday School program. We began to sense some reservation on the part of a few classes to utilize the lessons from the quarterly on stewardship. One teacher actually balked and complained that these lessons were timed only to help pay for future expansion. Our Sunday School director offered to provide another teacher as a substitute for those lessons. The original teacher became upset and resigned. We later found through dialogue with the class members that this gentleman had constantly used his platform to complain about the growth of the church. He quite openly admitted that he did not tithe and thus had no desire to teach on money. We found that this had created confusion for class members on this important biblical issue. You simply cannot teach that which you are unwilling to obey.

The teacher should be supportive of the mission and vision of the church. This is not to suggest that a teacher does not have the right to voice concern to church leaders in the proper forum, but it does mean that the teacher should not use the classroom to mount a rebellion against the direction of the church. Once the church has approved a particular plan or project, it is essential that the entire body move forward in unity.

The teacher will encourage class members to invite unsaved friends

It has been clearly shown that nothing is more effective in bringing unsaved persons to church than a personal invitation. If you expect to have non-Christian friends in your Sunday School class, the class members will have to invite them to attend. As a teacher, you can lead the way in this endeavor.

First, you can model this principle by bringing friends. Second, you can create an atmosphere of acceptance in the classroom that will help your class members feel comfortable in bringing their friends. You should think of such matters as how the chairs are arranged. Visitors often arrive late. Will they be required to walk into the room from the front? This can be most embarrassing for a first-time visitor, particularly a non-Christian. Do you have someone at the door whose assignment it is to make guests feel at home? Are chairs left near the back of the classroom for late arrivers? These are all small matters that can make the visitor have a good first-time experience. The teacher can ensure that the Sunday School class is "first-timer friendly." This attention to detail will encourage class members to bring friends.

The teacher should also prepare far enough in advance that he or she can tell class members if a particular lesson would be especially appropriate for visitors. For example, some lessons lend themselves to a clear gospel presentation. At other times, the lesson may cover a topic of particular interest. Lessons that address current issues are often very appealing to the non-Christian.

If the church body has determined to have a high-attendance emphasis or an "Invite a Guest" Sunday, the teachers in the classroom are the key to the success of such a program. As a teacher, you should promote such an emphasis with enthusiasm. This will actually give you the opportunity to teach the powerful Word of God to the unsaved guests.

The teacher will ensure that all class members receive appropriate ministry

The care ministry of the Sunday School class will never function effectively if it is not endorsed by the teacher. The teacher can emphasize the importance of the care leader and the care groups. He or she can lead the class to pray for one another. Some Sunday School classes may choose to have a class president or inreach leader take care of the opening period of the class. Even in these cases, the teacher's support of the care ministry program is pivotal to its success.

It is not expected, or appropriate, that the teacher provide the care for all the members, but the teacher must ensure that caring ministry is working effectively. If the teacher notices that a particular member has been absent for several Sundays, he or she might want to call the appropriate care leader and inquire about the welfare of the member. This will not only create accountability for care leaders, it will also encourage them to know that the teacher thinks their work is important. It is always appropriate for the teacher to call a member and inquire about needs and have prayer over the phone. A call or visit from the teacher will always have a great impact.

A caring teacher will be a great teacher, even if they are not strongly gifted in the area of teaching. I have asked numerous laypersons to name their favorite Sunday School teacher. After they name the teacher, I ask them why they chose this particular person. With few exceptions, their choice of a favorite teacher is based on an interpersonal relationship rather than teaching skill. People remember the teachers who took a personal interest and cared for them before they remember those who were gifted orators. You can be a great teacher if you will lead your class to be a caring class.

The teacher will interpret the work and vision of the church

As a pastor, I viewed my Sunday School teachers as staff. They were the extension of my pulpit and caring ministry. I knew that they had the opportunity to teach in a small-group setting where dialogue and sharing could take place. As a church grows larger, the pastor will have less and less opportunity to spend regular time in a small-group setting with all the members of the church. For that reason, I wanted my teachers to have a clear understanding of our purpose and vision. I knew that they would have a significant impact for good or ill in the communication of that purpose and vision.

As a teacher, you should relish the opportunity to assist your pastor and staff in clarifying the work and vision of the church. You can do this through a positive word of announcement where appropriate and by illustrating your Bible study from the things that God is doing in the life of the church. The teacher must communicate positively about the work of the church, or he or she will subtly undermine the effectiveness of the church and actually tear down the body. If you are in a situation where you find it difficult to speak a word that builds up the body, I would encourage you to seek an appointment with the pastor or other leader and resolve your concerns.

The teacher will give birth to a new class each year

Every class should have as its goal the birthing of a new class every year. This can demonstrate your effectiveness as a teacher and help the church fulfill its mission. As your class grows through the reaching of the unsaved, it will soon outgrow its ability to function effectively as a small group. I have found that classes that have had positive leadership from the teacher experience little or no trauma when they are called on to create a new teaching unit. In the ideal setting, the teacher should take the initiative in suggesting the need for a new teaching unit.

Many pastors and ministers of education tell me that the mere mention of creating a new unit throws the entire Sunday School into a traumatized situation. Cries of "don't split our class" are heard throughout the hallways. This can easily be avoided if teachers are recruited with the understanding that one of their goals is to grow their class to such an extent that it is necessary to give birth to a new unit. This should be viewed as a goal accomplished, not punishment for overachievement. It should be adopted as the standard for all Sunday School classes. Sunday School administrators should recognize those classes that reach this important growth goal.

We can learn a lesson from the human body. Healthy growth comes from cell division. When one cell becomes larger, you have a cancerous condition, not a healthy growth situation. Large, teacher-centered classes can often become a church within a church. They can provide an unhealthy forum for those who oppose growth and change. It is also important to note that cell division is initiated by the division of the nucleus of the cell. The teacher is nucleus of the Sunday School cell. The teacher should both promote and initiate cell division when necessary.

Teachers will reproduce themselves yearly

Every teacher should establish a goal to discover and mentor one new teacher yearly. It is a tragedy when a gifted teacher becomes selfish and is unwilling to send class members out to serve. It is the highest of compliments when a teacher is known for producing other teachers.

When a teacher notices that a class member is constantly well-prepared, freely enters into discussion, and shows spiritual maturity, he or she should encourage that individual to pray about the possibility of sharing in the teaching ministry of the church. If the person expresses interest, the teacher can introduce the individual to the Sunday School superintendent or pastor. The teacher should also begin to spend time with the potential teacher explaining various teaching procedures. It may be appropriate to invite the "teacher in training" to teach a portion of the lesson when the teacher is present. If the individual is prepared, the teacher might ask him or her to substitute teach on an occasion when the teacher cannot be present. It is often ideal that the teacher for the new unit actually comes from the class that is giving birth to the new unit. This provides for continuity and makes the separation less painful.

The Teaching Role

If you are a teacher, you are probably most interested in focusing on the teaching role. Let's address, from a practical standpoint, the most important issues you face as a teacher. This material will also be of interest to the pastor and Sunday School director as they administer the Bible teaching program.

Adequate preparation is essential

Anyone who has taught the Bible will readily admit that nothing can be accomplished without the empowering of the Holy Spirit. It is nonetheless interesting that the Holy Spirit uses most effectively those instruments that are most prepared for service. The work of the Spirit does not preclude the need for preparation. Preparation involves both the study of the biblical material with the accompanying tools (for example, a quarterly, commentary, and Bible dictionary) and also an understanding of the needs of the students.

Knowledge of the needs of the students can only be learned through class response, reports from care leaders, visitation, observation, and fellowship events. The understanding of the text and the understanding of the student needs must be bathed in prayer as one prepares for the next appointed hour of Bible study. We could represent the preparation formula thus:

$$\frac{\text{Prayer}}{\text{Knowledge of Student Needs + Understanding of Text}} = \frac{\text{Effective}}{\text{Teaching}}$$

Every teacher should take advantage of any regularly scheduled preparation meetings provided by the church (see chap. 9). The advantages of studying with other teachers are many. You can share ideas for illustration and application as well as obtain help with difficult interpretive issues. You will learn new teaching techniques and develop a team spirit.

As you prepare your lesson, you should keep in mind your general goals as well as specific outcomes. If you can't put into writing your goals as well as outcomes, it is unlikely that you will communicate them well in the classroom setting. You should be able to clearly articulate what a student should know and do as a result of this lesson. Knowing your goals and desired outcome will help you decide on the teaching approach for a given Sunday. On some occasions you might favor discussion over lecture. This will also help you know in advance how you want to arrange the room and whether any additional material and equipment will be needed for the teaching experience.

Use the Bible as your text

It should go without saying that the Bible is the textbook of the Sunday School. Yet that needs to be modeled by teaching from the Bible. I encouraged my Sunday School teachers to read the text from the Bible and not from the quarterly. The quarterly and other aids to Bible study must remain secondary. As noted already, people come to Sunday School to study the Bible.

The use of the Bible as a text will reinforce the use of the Bible for study at home. If you are concerned that some persons in attendance may not be familiar enough with the Bible to find the text, you can lead the entire class in a lighthearted look for the book. Let's take an example. One Sunday your lesson material is taken from Habakkuk. You might ask them to turn to the book as follows: "Our lesson today is from Habakkuk. I know it is often difficult to find some of the Old Testament books we don't use everyday, so let me offer some assistance. Let's turn together to the front few pages of the Bible. You will find there a listing of the books of the Bible. Look toward the end of the Old Testament listing and you will see a number of books with rather strange sounding names. These books are sometimes referred to as the minor prophets, not because of their message, but because of their length. You will find Habakkuk fifth from the end. You can locate it by turning to the page indicated in your Bible."

Use appropriate literature

Decisions about literature used in the Bible study program may be made for the teacher by the staff or board of the church, but there are issues worth discussing at this point. Whatever literature is chosen, it should meet certain minimum requirements.

1. Literature should be doctrinally sound. If it does not meet this criteria, little else matters.

2. Literature should be comprehensive. It should cover the entire Bible and major doctrines of the church over a specified time cycle.

3. Literature should be designed so as to communicate biblical content and to facilitate lifestyle change. If learning does not produce behavioral results, we have not completed our work.

4. Literature should be age appropriate.

5. Literature should include contemporary content and practical application.

6. Literature should be carefully designed so as to be easy for the student to study. If a teacher's quarterly is supplied, it should have teaching aids for the teacher.

7. Literature should be affordable.

Several options exist for the procurement of literature. The church could decide to write its own curriculum. This would be possible only for larger churches with sufficient staff to accomplish the work necessary. Even in those settings it is difficult to maintain the high quality desired with sufficient teaching helps. Few churches will find this to be satisfactory.

Some churches have attempted to use Christian books or study guides chosen on a quarterly basis. This strategy requires that someone be accountable for reviewing the content of books to be studied for doctrinal integrity and relevance. Further, this system does not build continuity and comprehensiveness into the Bible study program.

This strategy, which is becoming increasingly common, has another serious drawback for the evangelistic Sunday School. The use of a book or study course material in Sunday School can create a closed system and thus negatively impact attendance, particularly that of newcomers or non-Christians. Let me illustrate this point. You have chosen a study course book on prayer for your Sunday School class to use this quarter. You request members to buy a copy of the book so they can fill in blanks provided for inductive study. Once the study moves past the third or fourth week, it will become increasingly difficult for a newcomer to catch up with the material. This can have two detrimental effects. Regular members that miss for several consecutive weeks due to illness or vacation may choose not to return to Bible study until a new quarter commences. Second, regular attenders will cease to invite friends, realizing that it would be difficult for them to participate in the study after it has begun. Most quarterlies, on the other hand, are designed so that the lessons fit together in a comprehensive plan, yet can stand alone each week.

A number of churches have chosen nondenominational materials that can be used by most evangelical churches. If one selects this option, the material should be tested by the seven basic criteria discussed above. This option could ultimately weaken doctrinal integrity and would be the desired choice only if the denominationally prepared literature was deemed to be doctrinally unsound.

The best choice for most will be the use of material prepared by their denomination. Let me address this issue in greater detail.

Anne Boylan, in her history of the Sunday School movement, chronicles the development of denominational publishing houses. She notes that many denominations began to express concern about the doctrinal integrity of their literature when they determined that Sunday School had become a significant evangelistic tool. For example, she quotes the founder of the Methodist Episcopal Sunday School Union, who declares that their own publications should be used exclusively to teach the doctrines and practices of Methodism. In a similar fashion the organizers of the General Protestant Episcopal Sunday School Union appealed to members for support in order "to instruct her younger members in the nature of her own peculiar character and claims."[3]

The demand for doctrinal integrity led to the development of distinctive denominational publishing houses. Any publishing company that intends to sell to numerous denominational groups will of necessity seek the lowest common denominator of theological agreement. This will create compromise on distinctives like the meaning and mode of baptism, church polity, and other issues that are denominational distinctives.

A second concern that was addressed by denominational publishing houses was the matter of moral teaching. For example, during the 1830s some groups began to take clear-cut stands on the issue of slavery. The American Sunday School Union, the generic publisher of that day, was unwilling to take a strong stand on this moral issue. This prompted strong sectarian criticism of its publications.[4]

The moral issues of our day may differ from those of the 1830s, but the principle is the same. The publisher that is attempting to satisfy a broad constituency from many denominational groups will often avoid critical moral issues out of concern for broad acceptability.

Many persons today are bemoaning the lack of denominational loyalty. Some even speak of a postdenominational age. Tragically, we may have unwittingly cooperated in the demise of our own denominational distinctives by our selection of the lowest common denominator literature, which cannot by its nature emphasize doctrinal distinctives or denominational mission strategies.

My concern goes beyond denominational loyalty. Recent studies by Benton Johnson, Dean R. Hoge, and Donald A. Luidens and Roger Finke, and Rodney Stark clearly demonstrate that doctrinal integrity and a convincing apologetic are essential to stable church growth. They discovered that those denominations that allowed a weakening of spiritual convictions ultimately lost ground.[5] Since the Sunday School is integral to doctrinal instruction in the local church, I recommend that you should give your denominational publisher first chance. However, I would still suggest that you evaluate it by the seven criteria mentioned above.

Vary your teaching methods

People often ask whether Sunday School should be primarily lecture or discussion. The answer to that question may depend on the context of the group and the material. Some lessons that are heavily based on content may require more lecture time. Need- or issue-centered lessons may benefit from a discussion approach. Many senior adult classes may prefer a lecture format while young adults will generally prefer discussion.

Most teachers will find it helpful to vary their teaching methodology based on the understanding of the needs of the class. It may be necessary to use both lecture and discussion in the same lesson period. The teacher may use a lecture format to present the basic biblical truth. He or she may then switch to discussion for application. In some cases the teacher may divide the class into discussion groups, with each having a specific task. Good quarterlies should provide assistance in teaching methodology. Variety in teaching methodology is probably the best rule of thumb.

A few words of caution are in order. Use of the lecture format is never an excuse for inattention to the needs of the students. The lecture-oriented teacher must carefully watch the students and draw them back into the lecture when attention appears to be waning. No one should make the study of God's Word boring.

Those attempting to encourage discussion should avoid asking questions that appear to have a single right answer. For example, "Who knows the name of Moses' wife?" Open-ended or opinion questions should be asked. This encourages discussion. Discussion should not be allowed to degenerate into the sharing of opinions about the correct understanding of a passage. It is the teacher's duty to ensure that doctrinal integrity is maintained even in the discussion format.

Teachers should avoid asking people to read a passage of Scripture unless permission is asked prior to class. Many biblical words are difficult to pronounce and unannounced assignments of Scripture can create general uneasiness and create an embarrassing moment for member and visitor alike. The practice of taking turns reading Scripture usually results in a rather uninspired and uninspiring reading of God's precious Word. Better ways should be found to involve members.

Enlisting Teachers

In order for the Sunday School to continue to function as a church growth tool the number of teachers will need to increase. It is obvious that you cannot start new units without an adequate number of qualified leaders to staff both existing and new units. Nothing will destroy growth momentum more quickly than the lack of leadership.

If adequate leadership does not exist to staff for present needs, church members will begin to complain about the emphasis on outreach. They will argue that there aren't enough leaders to meet present needs, and then speculate about the problems the church would face if more people are reached. You've heard the refrain, "I don't know why we keep trying to reach these youth; we don't have enough teachers to care for the ones we have." The church then begins to become introverted, growth stops, and people begin to speculate about the lack of growth. This is the beginning of a stagnancy cycle that can lead more evangelistic members to leave the church out of frustration. The church can avoid this frustration by planning ahead for leadership needs.

Every church will need to develop its own strategy for recruitment based on policy and tradition. Some churches have committees that are responsible for teacher recruitment, others leave this task primarily to the staff or Sunday School leadership. Truthfully, teacher recruitment must become the concern of everyone in the Sunday School organization. Here are some basic principles to follow in recruiting teachers.

Pray to the Lord of the harvest

If your church has a leadership problem, it may actually be a prayer problem. Jesus told His disciples that the harvest was ripe, but the workers were few. He gave them the following instructions: "Therefore beseech the Lord of the harvest to send out workers into His harvest" (Matt. 9:38).

Make leadership recruitment a matter of churchwide prayer. Pray specifically! If you need five youth leaders by August 1, pray for five youth leaders by August 1. Those responsible for enlisting teachers should pray about persons before they attempt to enlist them. Pray for God to give you favor with those you plan to enlist to teach. Ask Him to create a receptive heart.

Personally enlist workers

Enlistment by announcement has little if any impact. The suggestion that we need "somebody" to work with our youth, usually means "somebody else." This sort of announcement is not only impersonal, it cheapens the task. When you have prayed about someone that you believe you should ask to teach or lead, visit that person personally. Explain how you arrived at his or her name, and ask if he or she will pray about this opportunity for ministry and give you an answer within the week. Pray with the person before you leave.

Call for commitment

Many churches have fallen into the trap of desperation enlistment. It sounds like this: "Please, you have to help us. We can't find anyone else for this class. You really don't have to do much. Just show up and teach about thirty minutes each week."

People God is calling to serve should be asked for a commitment. Do not be afraid to call for commitment. Leith Anderson notes that Baby Boomers tend to respond well to institutions that have high expectations of them.[6] Teaching the Bible is an investment in eternity. It should never be entered into lightly.

It is best to give the prospective teacher a job description when you ask him or her to pray about teaching. That job description should list expectations. If the person is expected to attend a weekly planning meeting, spell it out at this time. The discussion of the role of the teacher may help you design a job description that would work in your present context.

Exalt the work of the Sunday School

When people understand the crucial role of the Sunday School in kingdom advancement and the life of the church, they will want to be involved. People want to make a difference. If you can show them that they can impact eternity through their service in Sunday School, they will want to serve.

Start with those gifted to teach

Churches are beginning to focus more on using people according to their spiritual gifts. People will serve with greater passion and effectiveness in areas where they are most gifted.[7]

Ask teachers to enlist and train teachers

Your existing teachers are your best resource for discovering potential teachers. Often through class discussion the teacher will find those who regularly prepare their lessons and have a genuine interest in Bible study. If the teacher will nurture and mentor those potential leaders, they will be prepared to respond affirmatively when invited to teach. All adult teachers should be challenged to enlist one other teacher during the year.

George Barna determined through research that there are more than enough people willing to serve in leadership roles. They must be involved in a team ministry, given limits to avoid burnout, and trained by experience rather than lecture.[8]

Training Teachers and Leaders for Sunday School

The task of the Sunday School is too vital to leave training to chance. The church must have a strategy for ongoing training of Sunday School leadership, or the leadership pool will continue to shrink. People are more likely to serve if they know that the church will provide them the resources and necessary training. Jesus instructed His disciples before He sent them out into ministry (Matt. 10:5).

Proper enlistment: The key to training

Teachers should be invited to teach with the understanding that training is an integral component of the teaching task. You cannot expect good results if you change the job description after teachers are recruited. The teacher should know that the task of teaching the Bible is such an important role that it would be ill-advised to volunteer without a commitment to ongoing training.

Mentoring: The best model

On several occasions I have referred to Matthew 9 and 10. In chapter 10, Jesus instructed and sent His disciples into fields ripe for the harvest. What He asked them to do in 10:1 is precisely what He had been doing in their presence (see Matt. 9:35).

A living model is most instructive. When a teacher enlists another teacher and then explains how to outline a lesson and prepare to teach, the lesson sticks. If the mentoring teacher then allows the prospective teacher an opportunity to teach while the mentor is present, the lesson is more deeply imbedded. Immediate feedback can provide both affirmation and correction. Teaching as a partner of a more experienced teacher is invaluable.

Instruction on teaching fundamentals

Certain aspects of teaching can be taught in a classroom setting. Teachers should be taught how to prepare a lesson, how to write a teaching aim, how to illustrate and introduce the lesson, how to apply the lesson, how to encourage discussion, and how to call for commitment.

Another significant component of effective teaching is age-group awareness. Teaching methods will vary according to the age group being instructed. Numerous books are available to help the local church with teacher training. I would highly recommend *The Teaching Ministry of the Church* as a resource for teacher training in the local church. Included are chapters on planning to teach, as well as chapters on age-group specifics.

Ongoing training: A priority

No matter how thorough the training prior to teaching, every teacher will need and desire ongoing training. This can be accomplished as a part of the regular workers' meeting (chapter 9), and by special training events. The church may invite a special guest in for the weekend to work with Sunday School leaders. We sponsored an event called, "Midnight Madness," which lasted from 7:00 P.M. until midnight on a Friday night. We found that people would often commit more readily four or five hours of training at one burst than the same amount of time spread over five weeks. You may need to try several different times and formats for training until you find the one that best suits your church.

Denominational camps and seminars

Many denominations offer training opportunities at camps or in a retreat setting at the local church. Often these are provided at a minimal cost to the local church. Teachers not only learn from the instructors, they also learn from their colleagues.

Conclusion

Teaching is at the heart of the Bible study program of the local church. The teacher must also be the catalyst and leader who pulls together the Great Commission strategy of the Sunday School class. Every teacher should establish clear goals for his or her teaching ministry.

The church can use the goals mentioned in this chapter to establish a clearly articulated job description for teachers. This job description should be utilized both in the enlisting and training of teachers.

Too much is at stake in the teaching ministry of the church for us to take lightly the role of the teacher. The teacher is the key to the effective Great Commission Sunday School.

❧

NINE

Putting It Together—
Keeping It Working

*A*s head coach, it's my job to put people in an environment that allows them to be the best that they can be. The way to go about that—on and off the field—is: (1) give them responsibility, (2) let them know you care, and (3) guide them to make good decisions.[1]

If you are a Dallas Cowboy's fan, you may have mixed feelings about Jimmy Johnson. Many longtime fans couldn't forgive Johnson for replacing the beloved Tom Landry, and others just didn't like his style; but Cowboy politics aside, it was difficult to argue with his record and with the philosophy stated above. His advice about how to turn the Cowboys around would apply equally to the ongoing work of the Sunday School. If you can create an environment that allows people to be the best they can be, you will have a healthy organization.

In this final chapter I want to take all the various strands of the work of the Sunday School and weave them together into one strong rope. The Sunday School, if properly designed and maintained, with attention to the unique context of your church, can become an effective Great Commission tool for the twenty-first century.

Integrating the Work of the Class

The individual class is the most important single component of the Sunday School organization. If an individual class is ineffective, it weakens the entire structure, and it negates the work of the whole for those who participate in that class. It sounds hollow to tell people you have a caring Sunday School if they are not experiencing personal care in their class. Here are seven checkpoints for integrating and maintaining the work of the class.

Keep the Great Commission strategy balanced

The Sunday School class is more than a teaching unit; it is a tool for outreach, assimilation, and teaching. *You can incorporate the entire Great Commission strategy into a single organization, but you cannot do it in one hour.* You will not be able to accomplish all three of these functions in a single hour on Sunday morning. In the Sunday morning hour, you may include a time for sharing results of outreach and ministry needs, but the focus will clearly be on teaching. The work of assimilation, fellowship, and evangelism will occur outside the class and at times other than Sunday morning.

The teacher is the key to the effective functioning of the triune leadership team. The teacher must maintain the team spirit and keep the class involved in the Great Commission strategy. If the teacher sees his or her role as an invited guest lecturer with no connection to the further work of the class, assimilation and evangelistic activities will languish. The teacher should lead the leadership team through prayer, coordination, and inspiration.

There should be regular evaluation to ensure that the three elements of the work of the class are balanced. The teacher must ask critical evaluative questions. Are members bringing unsaved friends? Does the outreach team visit unsaved prospects regularly? Has anyone been led to Christ through the ministry of our class? Are members being contacted regularly? Are care needs being missed? Are members attending regularly? Are members frequently lost from the class? Why? Does the teaching address the spiritual needs of the class? Do members prepare for Bible study? Do they participate in class discussion?

Nothing is more important than what we do through the church, and therefore we must continually seek to strive for excellence. Continual evaluation and improvement of the integrated work of the Sunday School is essential.

Keep good records

I once read a story in the sports page about Michael Jordan, when he was in his early years with the Chicago Bulls. During a preseason, intersquad scrimmage, Jordan left the floor and took a seat on the sidelines. The press swarmed around him to determine what was wrong with the emerging superstar. He calmly remarked that he had quit the scrimmage because the coach had lost count of the score. The reporters responded that the score didn't matter in a preseason scrimmage. Jordan explained that there's no reason to play if you aren't going to keep score. He was driven to excellence and therefore the score was an indicator of how well he was doing.

You can't provide excellence in ministry if you don't keep good records. The parable of the shepherd and the ninety-nine sheep should become a model for the Sunday School class. The shepherd knew that a sheep was missing because he had numbered and counted them. Our purpose for keeping count of the sheep is to enable us to minister effectively to them.

Your record system should be built on the purpose of the Sunday School. Many denominations and independent publishers provide record-keeping material for the Sunday School. These can be used as they are printed or modified for your special needs. You should record only the material you intend to use and that will help you to accomplish your task. Asking for information that no one uses creates needless work and hinders the collection of relevant data.

You obviously need to know who is present or absent. You should keep track of attendance trends to assess the vitality of the class, but the critical need for attendance records relates to the caring side of the Sunday School. If there exists a chronic absentee pattern, the care leader should be informed. Such knowledge might prompt a visit in the home by the care leader and the teacher. Your goal is to faithfully fulfill the Great Commission through the Sunday School, not to win a high attendance award.

The records should also indicate the presence of visitors. These names should be given to the outreach leader for a follow-up contact. The attendance of visitors should be tracked until a connection is made with the class and ultimately a decision is made for Christ. The number and frequency of in-town visitors is important to track. It tells you how effective the class has been in inviting the unsaved. This information will assist the leadership team in evaluating class needs.

If your church gives the offering through the Sunday School, you may want to set class goals for giving and keep adequate records to evaluate the growth in stewardship. Any other data that will help you to evaluate the growth of believers and the ministry of the class should be kept and reviewed periodically.

Records of ministry and evangelistic visits are essential. Here again, we are not interested in numbers per se, but in ministry results. If the outreach leaders are connected to the larger outreach program of the church, then they will need to keep records of their visits for that program. They should also be allowed to report regularly to the class so they can share in the prayer needs and rejoice in the results.

The care leaders will need to report to the inreach leader so that ministry plans can be made and accountability can be maintained. The care leaders should report only those needs to the class that should be common knowledge, or those they have been given permission to share. For example, it would be perfectly normal to share the news of a hospital stay or a death in the family of a class member. More personal concerns that are not common knowledge should only be shared with the class or the staff when permission is given. If this confidence is not kept, the caring ministry will break down.

The class will not be successful in fulfilling its goals if it does not take seriously the matter of record keeping. Every class needs to find someone who sees this task as their calling and who is gifted as a helper.

Schedule regular fellowship outings

Fellowship outings tend to fall into two basic categories—planned and spontaneous. A planned event is scheduled, announced, organized, and publicized. It may focus around a particular theme, such as a picnic, a pool party, or a Valentine's dinner. You can let your imagination be your guide. If you have someone in the class who is particularly creative and has the gift of hospitality, you should put this person in charge of the planned fellowships. Attention should be given to the cost of outings so that no one will be excluded. Many of your fellowships will require little if any costs. You can have a dessert fellowship and ask everyone to bring their favorite dessert. Drinks can be provided by the host or hostess. In young-couples classes, you should also think about child care issues. You could plan some fellowships that would include the children, such as a pool party or an event at a local park.

Fellowships provide an opportunity to invite quests who may be reluctant to attend worship or Bible study. We found that fellowship events provided an excellent outreach opportunity. Every class should have a fellowship outing at least once a quarter.

Smaller, less formal gatherings should occur on a more frequent basis. Class members should be encouraged to go to Sunday lunch together on a regular basis. Spontaneous events can often be very effective because they require little planning or work on the part of anyone. Effort should be made to include newcomers in the informal events and to change the mix of the group in attendance. Often a few good friends will develop a pattern of going out together and it may become unintentionally exclusive in nature. This can actually harm the fellowship of the class.

Pay attention to the physical surroundings

The classroom should be prepared for Bible study prior to arrival on Sunday morning. The optimum situation is to have a classroom that is designed and built for Bible study for your age group. This room will have the proper size chairs, adequate room for the participants, marker boards, and other teaching tools as needed. Chairs should be arranged to facilitate the teaching style most appropriate to the lesson. If you plan to encourage discussion, you should arrange the chairs so that people can see one another. Attention should be given to various entry points into the room. You do not want late arrivers to be embarrassed by having to enter at the front of the class. This is particularly important in relationship to newcomers who may be late due to their unfamiliarity with the church building.

The classroom space should be well lit, bright, and freshly painted. The temperature of the room should be appropriately maintained. The appearance of the room will indicate the level of commitment you have to Bible study. Your Sunday School facilities must be well maintained. It does not require a large budget to ensure that the facilities are kept in good condition. The members of the church can be enlisted to do much of the upkeep of the church. Let class members paint their own room. This not only saves the church money, it involves the people, and it creates a sense of pride of ownership.

During a growth spurt, you can make temporary facilities work for you. We have had classes meeting in the kitchen, baptistry dressing rooms, and church offices. You can also use off-campus sites, such as restaurants and hotels. Yet attention should always be given to the appearance of the room and to its arrangement for the teaching task.

If you have organized your Bible study through home cell groups, you should still give careful attention to the appearance and arrangement of the space. Most cell groups will focus on a discussion method, therefore the room arrangement can be more casual. Locations should be chosen based on space, accessibility, and parking. You should be warned that some communities have ordinances that prohibit regular religious gatherings in the neighborhood. You should ask someone to advise you about local requirements.

Make sure guests are welcomed

We often fail to look at our class through the eyes of the newcomer. It can be intimidating to walk into a class of smiling, busily conversing strangers. The best alternative is for someone from the class to bring a guest to Bible study with them. This will make everyone most comfortable. However, when someone visits on their own, he or she still must be put at ease.

Every class should have someone at the door of the classroom to greet guests. This individual should have a name tag and some identification that he or she is there to serve. (Many classes will use name tags for everyone to facilitate name recognition for members and visitors.)

The individual who is assigned to greet guests should also introduce the newcomer to others in the classroom. Once class has begun, the greeter can be stationed near the door to assist those arriving late, pointing them to a seat and showing them what Scripture text is being studied. The class host or hostess should also take the initiative in ensuring that all guests are invited to sit with someone in the worship service.

Your attention to these details will not only assist you in the teaching task, it will indicate the importance of Bible study to the total life of the church. It will make your guests feel that they were expected and wanted.

Give birth to a new unit every year

Giving birth to a new teaching unit should not be seen as an option, but as a holy obligation. You should instill in every class the desire to see another teaching unit born every year because God has given divine increase through the work of the class. This should be an occasion for rejoicing. Classes should be recognized and affirmed when they accomplish this growth goal. Once every class develops a Great Commission mind-set, the creating of new units will become a natural and joyous occasion.

Since many churches struggle with the creation of new teaching units, let me give you six good reasons to prioritize the creation of new units on a regular basis.

1. The birth of new units create excitement.

2. The creation of new units enlarges the organizational base of the Sunday School, thus enabling it to grow naturally without sacrificing quality.

3. New units grow more quickly than older established units.

4. New units are easier for newcomers to penetrate. This aids in the assimilation of new members.

5. New units tend to be more evangelistic.

6. The creation of new units allows more people to serve in leadership positions.

Perhaps you are wondering how a church knows when to start new units. While the answer to this question may vary from church to church, here are some guidelines that can be used to help you determine when to start a new unit:

1. When the classroom has reached 80 percent of its capacity in regular attendance[2]

2. When relationships become strained

3. When a class outgrows its caring ministry

4. When better teaching will result

5. When competent leaders are available

Some churches make the mistake of creating new units without adequate planning. You should look ahead and have equipped leaders prior to the creation of a new unit. If you take persons from a class that is functioning properly with a balanced Great Commission strategy and place them in a class where the leaders are disorganized and unprepared, you can actually do more harm than good. You should enlist and train the teacher, the outreach leader, and the inreach leader before you start a new unit. I am not trying to delay the starting of new units; I am suggesting that you plan ahead.

We should probably answer one final question about new units: "How do I start a new unit?"

First, you must assess the area of need. Which class has become stagnant? What age group are we failing to reach? Questions such as these will help determine your need.

Second, you should pray about the need and ask the Father to provide the leadership.

Third, you should enlist the ministry team and provide the necessary training.

Finally, you must implement your strategy. Classes may be started in several different ways. You can divide an existing class that has become too large to minister. Sometimes you may find that it is better to reorganize an entire department. For example, the young adult department might presently have three classes. Rather than dividing one class, you may look at the age groupings and the potential for growth and then decide that to realign the department would require five classes. Each class would then provide members for the starting of the two new classes. Some churches actually start a paper class. They simply have a list of new prospects or church members who have not become involved in a small-group Bible study unit.

Ensure that classes remain small enough to minister

Most authors in the field of small-group dynamics agree that relationships in a small group begin to break down once a class reaches a regular attendance of fifteen. For this reason, most churches have utilized an enrollment goal of twenty-five to thirty for adult groups. Small-group dynamics and caring ministry are more difficult to achieve in larger groups. Nonetheless some churches are having success with larger classes. Kirk Hadaway's research indicated that growing churches have larger Sunday School classes than do plateaued or declining churches.[3]

We found that singles and college students enjoyed the excitement of the larger class. And our senior adults had such an effective care ministry that their attendance and enrollment could be above the norm without diluting their ministry. We also allowed couples classes to grow to double the normal enrollment since the caring contacts remained constant. One contact actually enables the care leader to minister to two persons.

If you choose to develop some larger classes, you should ensure that the caring ministry is expanded to maintain accountability and keep caring groups sufficiently small. You should also select teachers who are team players and use a variety of teaching methods. You may need to develop some larger classes to fully utilize the space that is available to you for Sunday School.

Larger classes do create some risks, and these should be understood and monitored. The larger class can become an entity unto itself and cease to cooperate with the task of the Sunday School. Some pastors have discovered that larger classes tend to become little congregations within the church.

Another pitfall is that the large class can take potential workers out of circulation. Often the larger class is taught by a very popular teacher.

People often become consumers in this setting and fail to become involved in the church's ministry. A final danger is that the larger class has a greater potential to become impersonal if caring ministry is not emphasized.

If you understand these pitfalls and work to avoid them, you may find that you can allow some classes to become somewhat larger than the norm. These large classes may allow a point of entry for those who may, at first, seek anonymity. The larger classes will probably always remain the exception rather than the norm. Here again you are in a position to be the judge of what size class will work best for you. You must customize your Sunday School so that it best serves your needs as you seek to fulfill the Great Commission.

Building the Church through the Sunday School

Let's turn our attention from the individual class to the entire Sunday School organization. Once you have taken the steps to organize the Sunday School based on the fundamental growth principles discussed in this book, with special attention to your own unique circumstances, you will need to give attention to keeping the Sunday School working on an ongoing basis. How do you avoid the stagnancy that tends to creep into every organization?

Nurture workers

Ministry is difficult at every level. The Sunday School, if utilized as a Great Commission tool, will place laypersons in critical ministry functions. This means that you must provide ongoing nurture and care for those who are doing the work of ministry.

Often we tend to overlook the spiritual needs of those in the trenches where the spiritual warfare is taking place. If you fail to provide this ministry, these persons will ultimately burn out. When burnout occurs leaders may actually leave the church out of embarrassment.

Schedule a regular workers meeting

Many churches have found a weekly workers meeting to be essential for coordination, planning, encouragement, and communication. If the weekly meeting proves to be unworkable in your setting, you could try to meet every two weeks or once a month. I would be reluctant to meet any less frequently than once a month, and I actually prefer the weekly meeting.

A key to regular attendance at the meeting is that you recruit teachers with the understanding that attendance is expected. You will find that many persons actually respond positively to the greater level of demand. Most churches would not consider having a choir that did not gather for rehearsal. They would be ill prepared to lead in worship. In similar fashion, it is difficult to think that we would entrust the teaching of God's Word to persons who did not have the commitment to meet for planning and prayer.

A second key is to make the meeting worth attending. People are busy and they establish priorities based on productivity. If you can demonstrate to your leaders that attendance at the workers meeting will actually save them time each week, you will have good results.

Each church will need to determine the most appropriate time for the meeting in its given context. Some have chosen to meet on Sunday before the evening service. In churches without a Sunday evening service, the workers meeting could utilize that time slot. Other churches have utilized Wednesday evenings. Some churches have actually provided alternative times because of scheduling conflicts. You alone can judge the best time for your church. You can also provide cassette recordings of the meetings for those who have to miss because of a conflict.

While there are numerous guides for how to conduct the workers meeting, you should feel free to make your meeting serve the needs of your church. You will not have any difficulty filling the hour with productive work. Here are a few elements you may want to consider.

Bring all the Sunday School workers together for a general period. This should be brief, five to fifteen minutes, led by the pastor, Sunday School director, or minister of education. This time should be used for general announcements, the good news of the past Sunday's records, and prayer for tonight's meeting. If someone has a particularly exciting testimony about outreach, care ministry, or teaching, he or she should be encouraged to share it during this time.

After the general time it is usually advisable to break into departmental groups. Each department director will lead respective groups. If you choose to bring care leaders, teachers, and outreach leaders together in this session, you should give them a time for sharing and praying.

The department meeting will then be broken into the three ministry groups. The department director should lead the teachers in a review of next week's lesson. He may also utilize some of the time for suggestions for improving teaching. The department deacon or inreach leader should meet with the care leaders to review needs and to provide ongoing training.

Often the care leaders will have time to begin their work. They can review the attendance records, write notes to absentees, etc. The outreach teams will often use this time for ongoing evangelism training.

I offer the above only as suggestions. You must design the time period to meet your church's needs. The workers meeting also provides an opportunity for the workers to receive ministry. Make it an exciting, inspirational, encouraging, and profitable time and your leaders will attend.

Promote members on a regular basis

Since most classes tend to reach their maximum growth potential in a relatively short period of time, regular promotion or reorganization will assist in growth. The Bible study organization has a natural tendency to stagnate. The stagnant class is difficult to penetrate, therefore it becomes difficult to assimilate new members.

Promotion functions more easily if the Sunday School is organized on the age-grading principles espoused in this book. If you have chosen another method for organization, such as topic or interest grading, you will still need to find some reorganization method for counteracting stagnancy in the small-group structure.

Most churches have found that promotion, as a strategy of reorganization, works best if it is maintained as an annual event. Most youth and children's classes are reorganized in conjunction with the beginning of the new school year. We found it most efficient to promote all age groups on the same day, but others have used a staggered promotion system. It is easier to promote at the beginning of a new segment of study so that there is both closure and an opportunity for a new beginning.

You will likely encounter some resistance to promotion among a few of the adult groups. This resistance is similar to that encountered in the starting of new units. The solution to this problem is essentially the same. You must first build a team spirit that is based on a Great Commission consciousness and an understanding of basic growth principles. The second key to successful promotion will be the adult teachers, therefore they should understand their role in this key issue of effective Sunday School growth. Third, you must communicate positively and frequently about the many advantages of promotion. You can make promotion Sunday an exciting event.

Most churches discover that they may encounter one or two teachers who have determined that they must hold onto their class members. They are negative about annual promotion and discourage their class members from participating. How do you handle this problem? You may find that in some cases you simply allow time to bring this class into line with the rest of the Sunday School structure. If the class in question is a holdout from the age-grading strategy of the Sunday School, you simply set them aside in the organizational chart and develop a complete age-grading system. They will either find it necessary to adapt to age grading or they will slowly decline as members move away or drop out.

If the difficulty arises with an age-graded class, you can ultimately resolve the problem as the classes on either side of them work within the system. You will promote enough new members into this class that the complexion of the group will begin to change. In some extreme cases you might need to replace the teacher. This must be done with caution and love, particularly in the smaller church where the teacher has been in place for a period of time. One or two uncooperative classes need not wreck the system or cause you not to do that which is best for the Sunday School.

Keep an adequate worker-to-pupil ratio

The ratio of workers to pupils is an important one because it will ultimately impact both the quality of the Sunday School ministry and its continued growth. If the ratio becomes too low, the caring ministry will suffer and people will become less active or totally drop out. The other downside to an inappropriately low ratio of workers to pupils will be the burnout rate among Sunday School workers. The teacher, care leaders, and outreach leaders, if not given sufficient help, will become discouraged and may ultimately resign.

Some Sunday School growth consultants argue that the Sunday School should aim for an overall ratio of one worker per ten persons enrolled. Obviously the younger classes will require a greater concentration of workers. The Sunday School structure that I recommend will easily maintain this ratio when you take into account the care leaders, teacher, and outreach leaders.

Another way to determine if you are adequately staffed is to follow the ratio of teachers to pupils by specific age-group needs. The younger the age group, the smaller the ratio must be. Suggested target ratios for preschoolers up to five years of age is one worker per four students. The ratio for children in grades one to six, and the ratio for youth in grades seven to nine, is one to ten. Youth grades ten to twelve is one to fifteen, while adult will be one to twenty-five. Remember these are ratios for teachers to students only. If you add care leaders or department workers, you should find that you will have a one-to-ten, or better, ratio for the entire Sunday School.

You can use either formula to evaluate your Sunday School needs. These should be used as guidelines, but they will need to be adapted to your unique situation. These guidelines should never be used as an excuse not to grow, but as a challenge to excellence.

Set and publicize goals

I sometimes encounter people who want to argue that goals are not spiritual and that the Sunday School should not focus on numerical goals. This argument is often a simple excuse for not reaching people. Goals aid in motivation and evaluation. Goals help us know what our aims are and whether we are accomplishing those aims.

I discovered the power of goals early in my work at First, Norfolk. Soon after I accepted the pastorate, the Sunday School superintendent and I attended a conference on the work of the Sunday School. The speaker encouraged us to adopt an annual goal for Sunday School enrollment. That year we adopted a bold, some would have thought foolish, goal. Each class set their own goal and then we added the class goals to create a goal for the entire Sunday School. To reach our goal we had to increase enrollment by a large percentage. We publicized the goals and regularly reminded the classes of their goals and their progress. As the year progressed, excitement grew as we crept toward an unthinkably large goal. By the end of the year we were able to celebrate the largest annual growth rate in the history of the church.

Good goals should be challenging enough to create excitement, require work, and demand prayer. They should be set by the class leaders so that each class has a sense of ownership.

Goals must be clearly publicized and regularly reviewed. If no attention is given to the progress being made toward a goal, people will become apathetic. When goals are reached, you should celebrate with the entire congregation.

Give appropriate recognition

People respond well to affirmation. We often ask people to do a job and then fail to thank them for their work. Appropriate gratitude is essential to the Christian life and to the effective work of the church. Many churches have recognition banquets to honor workers in Sunday School. This should be a special evening that is paid for through the budget if sufficient resources are available.

When an individual or a class provides the leadership that enables the Sunday School to fulfill its purpose, it is appropriate to recognize them before the entire church family. Let me give you an example. Due to growth, it was necessary for us to create a third Sunday School at 8:15. As we began to develop the classes for the early hour, a teacher came to me on behalf of his class and volunteered to move to the first Sunday School. This generous gesture was all the more impressive when you take into account that this was a class of young adults with preschool children.

On the Sunday before the move, I asked the teacher and the entire class to stand during the worship service. I told the church about the level of sacrifice this class was making to help the church reach lost people through the Sunday School. This simple act not only affirmed this class, but it prompted other classes to move to the earlier hour.

I would encourage you to affirm those actions that help the Sunday School to achieve its Great Commission purpose. If you recognize those classes that have the largest attendance, you can actually discourage teachers from creating new units or promoting adults. If you recognize those classes that have the greatest percentage of members present, you often encourage teachers to drop inactive members rather than to minister to them. Thus you should affirm those teachers who lead their classes to give birth to a new teaching unit. Recognize those teachers who have the most members teaching in other classes in the Sunday School. You can give affirmation to the evangelistic outreach of the Sunday School by having someone from the appropriate class stand with new converts from their class when they are being presented to the church. People will respond to those actions that are affirmed by the pastor and the church.

Make your Sunday School visitor-sensitive

I have addressed the matter of visitor sensitivity as it relates to the individual class, but now I would like to focus on the entire Sunday School. Every church will need to customize the suggestions made here to the needs and resources of their own church.

• Provide parking places near the most visible entry of the church. These should be clearly marked so that the first-time visitors can see them as they enter the parking lot. Larger churches often will have parking attendants and will place a sign at an entry point requesting visitors to turn on their headlights. The parking attendant will then direct them to visitor parking and welcome guests to the church.

• Develop a plan for welcoming visitors as they enter the church. You should have greeters at every door. The greeters should be clearly identified with a badge or name tag. Greeters should welcome everyone to church, but they should also be prepared to offer special assistance to visitors.

• Consider establishing a welcome center. The visitor may not be familiar with the language of the church or the location of appropriate rooms. If you have an appropriate room near the entry, you should use it. If no room is available, you can build a cart that will enable you to meet the visitors' immediate needs. In a welcome center, you can provide coffee and juice and have hosts and hostesses to make visitors feel at home. You can assist your guests by filling out visitors' cards or enrollment forms while they are in the welcome center.

• Your guests should be taken to the appropriate Sunday School classes. In the case of a family, you should first escort the family to the appropriate preschool or children's classes so that the parents can meet the teacher and be familiar with the class location. The host or hostess should then take them to the appropriate adult class and introduce them to someone in the class.

Combine open enrollment with personal contact

Open enrollment means you are prepared to enroll people in your Sunday School at any appropriate opportunity. Many churches have developed a small enrollment card the size of a business card. This small size encourages members to keep the card with them at all times. I have actually enrolled persons while visiting with them in a restaurant. We often enrolled persons during the follow-up visit in the home. You can add an additional blank to the visitor card you use during the worship service, asking people to "check here" if they would like to be enrolled in small-group Bible study.

Some people argue against open enrollment because they see it as a way of inflating the numbers of people involved in the Sunday School. This can be true if those enrolled are not ministered to through the Sunday School. Open enrollment is not a magic formula for church growth. The purpose of open enrollment is to develop a ministry opportunity with a large number of people through the Sunday School. You should assign everyone enrolled to a care group and then provide regular ministry.

Stress excellence

The Great Commission Sunday School should keep its focus on excellence in teaching, outreach, and ministry. This can only be accomplished when everyone understands the purpose of the Sunday School and works together to accomplish the appropriate goals. Accountability and ongoing training will enable you to emphasize quality while you reach, teach, and minister to large numbers of people.

Innovate without compromising the basics

I have continually emphasized the need to contextualize the Sunday School to meet your unique situation and needs. Innovation is always built on the foundation of the basics. Learn the basic growth principles and then build on them with innovative strategies that will enable you to best accomplish your goals in your community. Don't be afraid to try new things even if some of them fail to work as you expected. Keep working with the basic principles in mind and you will find how you can best use your Sunday School to help grow the church.

Creatively Providing Space

As your Sunday School grows, space issues will constantly confront you. If you are reaching young couples, you will find that the preschool space will need to be expanded constantly. Adults will be more flexible about their own classroom space if they are confident that their children are well cared for. If you fail to provide adequate space, the Sunday School growth you are experiencing will slow down and ultimately cease.

The basic needs

In *The Bonsai Theory of Church Growth,* I discuss the 80-percent rule. When attendance in any room surpasses 80 percent of the capacity of that room, attendance growth will slow, plateau, and then decline until it ultimately settles in at 80 percent of available space. That means that if a classroom could accommodate twenty adults, it will slow in growth as it reaches sixteen. It may then grow slowly toward nineteen or twenty but it will not maintain 100 percent attendance. Attendance will vacillate around the sixteen mark while enrollment will continue to grow. We could illustrate this phenomenon as follows:

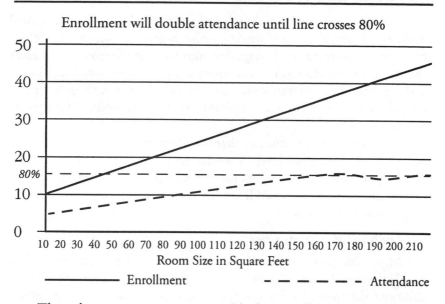

Enrollment will double attendance until line crosses 80%

————— Enrollment   – – – – – – Attendance

The only way you can counteract "the bonsai effect" is to begin a new class or to move the existing class to a larger room.

The growing Sunday School must be proactive in dealing with the need for space. You should constantly monitor space needs and have a plan in mind as a particular class approaches the 80-percent ceiling. If you do not act soon after 80-percent capacity is reached, you will lose momentum.

It is easier to move a class or to create a new unit when the class is experiencing strong growth than when it has already plateaued. The plateaued classes will often argue that they still have a few empty chairs and that they have been able to seat more people in the past.

Let me suggest some rough square-footage numbers to help you determine the saturation point for the various age groups in the Sunday School. In the preschool area, you need approximately thirty-five square feet per child for very young preschoolers. This may seem excessive, but you need to keep in mind that preschoolers do not sit still for very long. You will need to have various learning centers in the classroom. If you violate these space parameters for extended periods, you will discover that you will experience a high level of turnover among preschool workers. In the children's division you need approximately twenty-five square feet per child, and in the youth divisions you will need to provide about ten to fifteen square feet per student. In the adult area you will need about ten square feet per member.

I recommend that every church take the floor plan of the educational building and mark it so as to determine the saturation level for every class-room based on the square-footage demands listed above. You should place two numbers in each room—one shows the 80 percent saturation figure and the other the maximum capacity of the room. You can total the figures on your floor plan and determine what you can accommodate in the entire Sunday School.

Many churches will discover that their Sunday School attendance has been over the saturation level on several occasions but that it has stalled and dropped back to that saturation point. This is a sure sign that addi-tional space must be provided if the Great Commission Sunday School is to continue to function.

Finding off-campus space

Many churches have found that off-campus space can be utilized to enable the church to continue to grow. You will need to determine the suit-ability of the space, its distance from the church, and which age group could most easily adapt to the space available.

As a rule of thumb, space that requires participants to move their cars will become cumbersome over an extended period of time. It can, however, be used as a stopgap measure to buy time so that a long-term solution can be found. You will also discover that adults who have young children will find off-campus space difficult to use.

Churches have had good success with youth, college-age adults, and singles without children in off-campus locations. Our singles found that some of their unsaved friends would more readily attend Bible study for the first time in a neutral sight than in an on-campus sight.

You should look for restaurants, motels, hospitals, office buildings, and schools that may be within walking distance of the church. All of these have large rooms that can accommodate a small-group Bible study. If these build-ings are owned by church members, you may find that the space can be used at no cost. If you are required to rent the space, make sure that you sign a lease that specifies both the time and the room that you will use. You don't want students to arrive only to discover that their room in a local motel has been given to another function and they have been moved to the lobby.

When looking for off-campus space, you might want to consider add-ing cell groups that meet in the home at an alternative time. I earlier dis-cussed the possibility of mixing cells and Sunday School. The saturation of the building might provide an excellent opportunity to begin cell groups.

If you currently do your Bible study through cell groups, you will still need to monitor the space issue and start new cells as existing ones saturate. The cell-designed church might want to also consider adding some Sunday morning cells at the church to accommodate young couples with small children.

Whether you prefer the cell approach or the Sunday School approach to Bible study, you must carefully monitor the space issue and continue to provide adequate space for growth to occur.

Consider using multiple Sunday Schools

The cheapest and most readily available solution to the space crunch is multiple Sunday Schools in the same space. No commandment exists that mandates that the Sunday School space can only be used once on a Sunday morning. Multiple Sunday Schools can be a positive solution to the space problem.

First, it is simply good stewardship. The Sunday School space will require heating and cooling for the entire period that folk are in the building whether they are used or not.

Second, the more time options you offer today, the more opportunities you have to reach the diverse population groups that live around your church. Some people's schedules do not allow them to attend Sunday School when it is scheduled. When you use dual Sunday Schools, you may open an avenue of opportunity for those who once had no opportunity to attend Sunday School.

The leaders of the local church will be best able to determine when the second Sunday School should be offered. Factors like the size of the sanctuary must be figured into the equation. In cases where the sanctuary is significantly larger than the Sunday School space, you could have Sunday School, worship, and Sunday School. Your schedule might look as follows:

8:30– 9:30 Sunday School

9:45–10:45 Worship

11:00–12:00 Sunday School

If Sunday School space and worship space are equally matched, you can simply alternate the two or flip-flop the Sunday School and worship time. Half the congregation would attend Sunday School before church, and the other half would attend worship first. Here is a possible schedule:

9:30—10:30 Sunday School and worship

11:00—12:00 Sunday School and worship

The permeations on Sunday morning are numerous. For example, you could have three Sunday Schools and two worships or three Sunday Schools and three worship services.

8:00— 9:00 Sunday School and worship
9:30—10:30 Sunday School and worship
11:00—12:00 Sunday School and worship

You must adapt these suggested schedules to meet the style of your church. If your worship service is normally longer than one hour, then you must adjust the schedule to fit your needs.

A word of caution! The more times you use the building, the greater the amount of time that you will need to leave for moving people from Sunday School to worship. People don't mind being crowded as much as they mind being rushed and herded along. You will also have to deal with issues like people movement and bathroom facilities as you use your buildings for multiple services.

The use of dual Sunday Schools will allow the Sunday School to grow to a size about 60 percent larger than the single Sunday School. Don't be fooled into thinking that you have the space to double attendance with the implementation of two Sunday Schools. Sixty percent will prove a good rule of thumb because you will be required to utilize more space for pre-schoolers at both hours since most preschoolers do not attend worship.

Build more space to fulfill the Great Commission

Building is never easy or inexpensive. It is hard work to build additional facilities for Sunday School or worship. Nevertheless it must be done if we are to be obedient to the Great Commission. We cannot allow cost or inconvenience to hinder the church from being obedient to the Great Commission. Building should never be seen as an end in and of itself; church buildings are nothing more than a tool enabling the church to fulfill the Great Commission. It was never my goal to build a building. It was always my goal to be obedient to the Great Commission. Always tie your building needs to your Great Commission strategy.

When you prepare to build, I would recommend that the church employ both a good architect and a good church-growth specialist. You need someone to look at the potential floor plan who understands the dynamics of church growth. This person can help you look at issues like people movement and size of classrooms as they relate to your educational philosophy. A poorly designed building can actually be a detriment to growth.

Conclusion

Your Sunday School can prove to be the unifying church growth tool you need. You must keep the focus and purpose of the Sunday School in mind as you develop and implement classes. Every teacher, care leader, and outreach leader must understand the overarching task of the class and the Sunday School program as it relates to the Great Commission. You must continually nurture the workers, communicate priorities, set appropriate goals, monitor those goals, stress excellence, recruit and train leaders and workers who are team players, and provide space for growth.

Don't be afraid to draw outside the lines. Once you understand the basics, you will need to contextualize the Sunday School to fit the unique needs of your church.

Your Sunday School has great potential if you will simply resurrect the dinosaur. Build on the great basics! Innovate to meet your unique needs! Build a strategy for the end of this century and beyond! Remember, it is God who works through us to grow His Church.

ë

Because we believe Bible study to be essential for the growth and maturity of every Christian, and because First Baptist Church places great importance on Bible study, every member is enrolled in the class or department of their choice. Bible study is offered every Sunday morning at 8:00, 9:30, & 11:00 A.M.

Your Sunday Bible study class is: _____

which meets at_____A.M. in room _____

The teacher is _____

Appendix

Generation X

Bernardi, Janet, and William Mahedy. *A Generation Alone: Xers Making a Place in the World.* Downers Grove, Ill.: InterVarsity Press, 1994.

Young Adult

Atkinson, Harley, ed. *Handbook of Young Religious Education.* Birmingham: Religious Education Press, 1995.

Baby Boomers

Barna, George. *The Barna Report: What Americans Believe.* Ventura, Calif.: Regal Books, 1991.

Bast, Robert L. *The Missing Generation: The Church's Ministry with the Baby Boom.* New York: Reformed Church in America and Church Growth, Inc., 1991.

Bell, James. *Bridge Over Troubled Water: Ministry to Baby Boomers: A Generation Adrift.* Wheaton, Ill.: Victor Books, 1993.

Jones, Landon Y. *Great Expectations: America and the Baby Boom Generation.* New York: Ballantine Books, 1981.

Murren, Doug. *The Baby Boomerang: Catching Baby Boomers as They Return to Church.* Ventura, Calif.: Regal Books, 1990.

Towns, Elmer L. *An Inside Look at Ten of Today's Most Innovative Churches.* Ventura, Calif.: Regal Books, 1990.

Agers

Hauk, Gary. *Building Bonds between Adults and Their Aging Parents.* Nashville: Convention Press, 1986.

Hendricks, William. *A Theology for Aging.* Nashville: Broadman, 1986.

&

Endnotes

Chapter 1

1. Anne M. Boylan, *Sunday School: The Formation of an American Institution, 1790* (New Haven: Yale University Press, 1988), 6.

2. Ibid., 7–9.

3. Ibid., 133–134.

4. Ibid., 78.

5. Quoted in J. N. Barnette, *A Church Using Its Sunday School* (Nashville: The Sunday School Board of the Southern Baptist Convention, 1937), 17.

6. Ibid., 17–18.

7. Arthur Flake, *Building a Standard Sunday School* (Nashville: The Sunday School Board of the Southern Baptist Convention, 1922), 106.

8. Delos Miles, *Church Growth: A Mighty River* (Nashville: Broadman, 1981), 83–106.

Chapter 2

1. Boylan, *Sunday School,* 39.

2. Quoted in Barnette, *A Church Using Its Sunday School,* 95.

3. Robert E. Logan, *Beyond Church Growth* (Tarrytown, N. Y.: Fleming H. Revell Company, 1989), 128.

4. Statistics from Uniform Church Letter provided by BSSB.

5. Kennedy Smartt, "Evangelism through Sunday Schools," in Roger S. Greenway, ed., *The Pastor-Evangelist* (Phillipsburg, N. J.: Presbyterian and Reformed Publishing Company, 1987), 106.

6. Kirk Hadaway, *Church Growth Principles: Separating Fact from Fiction* (Nashville: Broadman, 1991), 40.

7. Leith Anderson, *A Church for the 21st Century* (Minneapolis: Bethany House, 1992), 61.

8. Elmer Towns, *154 Steps to Revitalize Your Sunday School and Keep Your Church Growing* (Wheaton: Victor Books, 1988), 41.

9. George Barna, *What Americans Believe* (Ventura: Regal Books, 1991), 263.

10. Joseph Allen Dennis, "Building Bridges to Baby Boomers through the Sunday School," (A Doctor of Ministry Project, Fuller Theological Seminary, 1993), 19.

11. Win Arn, *The Church Growth Ratio* Book (Pasadena, Calif.: Church Growth, 1987), n.p.

Chapter Three

1. Barnette, *A Church Using Its Sunday School*, 31–32.

2. For a more detailed discussion for how the church can experience this supernatural empowering please see the first three chapters of Ken Hemphill, *The Antioch Effect* (Nashville: Broadman & Holman, 1995).

3. Kennedy Smartt's article is found in Roger S. Greenway, ed., *The Pastor-Evangelist* (Phillipsburg, N. J.: Presbyterian and Reformed Publishing Company, 1987).

4. Logan, *Beyond Church Growth*, 66.

5. Benton Johnson, Dean R. Hoge, and Donald A. Luidens, "Mainline Churches: The Real Reason for Decline," *First Things: A Monthly Journal of Religion & Public Life* (March 1993): 15.

6. Roger Finke and Rodney Stark, *The Churching of America 1776–1990* (New Brunswick, N. J.: Rutgers University Press, 1992), 1.

Chapter 4

1. Ken Hemphill, *The Bonsai Theory of Church Growth* (Nashville: Broadman & Holman, 1991).

2. Several tools that may be helpful in establishing and communicating vision are: Robert Dale, *To Dream Again* (Nashville: Broadman, 1981); George Barna, *The Power of Vision* (Regal Books, 1992); and chapter 6 of my book, *The Antioch Effect* (Nashville: Broadman & Holman, 1994).

3. I have recently developed a new training module for discovering spiritual gifts entitled *Serving God: Discovering and Using Your Spiritual Gifts*. It is available from Sampson Ministry Resources, 5050 Quorum Drive, Suite 245, Dallas, Texas 75240.

4. Richard Beckhard, *Changing the Essence* (San Francisco: Jossey-Bass, 1992).

Chapter 5

1. Flake, *Building a Standard Sunday School*, 49.

2. Ibid., 50.

3. Barnette, *A Church Using Its Sunday School*, 149–150.

4. Rick Warren, *The Purpose Driven Church* (Grand Rapids: Zondervan Publishing House, 1995), 81.

5. J. N. Barnette, *The Pull of the People* (Nashville: Broadman, 1953), 42–43.

6. Flake, *Building a Standard Sunday School*, 51–53.

7. Dennis Allen, *Building Bridges to Baby Boomers through the Sunday School* (Ann Arbor, Mich.: UMI Dissertation Services, 1994), 19–20.

8. Flake, *Building a Standard Sunday School*, 49 and 59.

9. "How Small Groups Are Transforming Our Lives," adapted from a study by Robert Wuthnow, *Christianity Today*, 7 February 1994, 20.

10. Charles Arn, "Small Groups . . . Ally or Adversary?" *The Growth Report*, n. d.

11. J. Maroney and Ralph Neighbor, *Cell Groups in Church Growth* (Richmond, Va.: The Foreign Mission Board of the Southern Baptist Convention, 1987), 6.

12. Ibid., 10.

13. Ibid., 6.

14. Ibid., 20.

15. Wuthnow, "How Small Groups Are Transforming Our Lives," 23.

16. George Barna, *Virtual America: What Every Church Leader Needs to Know about Ministry in an Age of Spiritual and Technological Revolution* (Ventura, Calif.: Regal Books, 1993), 52–55. Warren Bird relates to Barna's study in "The Great Small Group Takeover," *Christianity Today,* 7 February 1994, 29.

17. Logan, *Beyond Church Growth*, 124.

18. Ibid., 123.

19. Ibid., 128.

20. Statistic supplied by Cliff Tharp, Strategic Information Unit of the Baptist Sunday School Board, Nashville, 20 September 1995.

Chapter 6

1. For a more complete discussion of the evangelistic Sunday School, you might want to read *Growing an Evangelistic Sunday School,* Ken Hemphill and R. Wayne Jones (Nashville: Broadman, 1989).

2. Hadaway, *Church Growth Principles,* 79–80.

3. Boylan, *Sunday School,* 168.

4. Ibid., 135–138.

5. Charles S. Kelley, *How Did They Do It?* (Insight, 1993), 89.

6. Hadaway, *Church Growth Principles,* 39–44.

7. Leith Anderson, *Dying for Change* (Minneapolis: Bethany House, 1990), 65.

8. Curt Dodd, *Hearts on Fire* (Denver: Accent, 1989), 69.

9. Kelley, *How Did They Do It?* 97.

10. If you are just beginning a visitation program, you might find it helpful to read *Going. . . One on One,* Harry Piland, compiler, with Ronald K. Brown (Nashville: Convention Press, 1994).

11. In most years, less than one third of all Southern Baptist churches indicate that they have any form of visitation program. I have treated the importance of visitation in greater detail in *The Antioch Effect,* 173.

Chapter 7

1. William Crabb and Jeff Jernigan, *The Church in Ruins* (Colorado Springs: NavPress, 1991), 45.

2. Lyle E. Schaller, *Assimilating New Members* (Nashville: Abingdon, 1978), 16.

3. Ibid., 49–51.

4. Schaller, *Assimilating New Members,* 21–22.

5. Hadaway, *Church Growth Principles,* 145.

6. Ibid., 145.

7. Gary McIntosh and Glen Martin, *Finding Them, Keeping Them* (Nashville: Broadman & Holman, 1994).

8. Schaller, *Assimilating New Members,* 16.

9. Hadaway, *Church Growth Principles,* 141.

10. For a more complete discussion of the discipling hierarchy, see my book *The Antioch Effect,* chap. 8.

Chapter 8

1. Marion E. Brown and Marjorie G. Prentice, *Christian Education in the Year 2000* (Valley Forge, Penn.: Judson Press, 1984), 48.

2. See the excellent chapter on "The Role of the Holy Spirit in Teaching," in Daryl Eldridge, ed., *The Teaching Ministry of the Church* (Nashville: Broadman and Holman, 1995).

3. Boylan, *Sunday School,* 78.

4. Ibid., 80.

5. Benton Johnson, Dean R. Hoge, and Donald A. Luidens, "Mainline Churches: The Real Reason for Decline," *First Things: A Monthly Journal of Religion & Public Life* (March 1993), and Roger Finke and Rodney Stark, *The Churching of America 1776* (New Jersey: Rutgers University Press, 1992).

6. Leith Anderson, *Dying for Change* (Minneapolis: Bethany House, 1990), 85.

7. Numerous gift inventories are now available. I have recently developed an open-ended inventory that is keyed to service opportunities available in the church. *Serving God: Discovering and Using Your Spiritual Gifts*

is available from Sampson Ministry Resources, 5050 Quorum Drive, Suite 245, Dallas, Texas, 75240.

8. George Barna, *The Frog in the Kettle* (Ventura, Calif.: Regal Books, 1990), 149.

Chapter 9

1. Jimmy Johnson, "Secret for Turning the Cowboys Around," in *Parade*, 15 August 1993, 5.

2. For information on space constraints see Ken Hemphill, *The Bonsai Theory of Church Growth* (Nashville: Broadman, 1994) chapter 1.

3. Kirk Hadaway, *Church Growth Principles: Separating Fact from Fiction* (Nashville: Broadman Press, 1991), 59.

੨ঌ